The Descent of the Dove

A SHORT HISTORY OF THE HOLY SPIRIT

by

Charles Williams

Printed on acid free ANSI archival quality paper.
ISBN: 978-1-78139-822-7.
© 2017 Benediction Classics, Oxford.

For the Companions of the Co-inherence

CONTENTS

PREFACE

My first intention for the title of this book was *A History of Christendom* : it was changed lest any reader should be misled. It is open to any reader to complain that many names, of persons and events, which have been of immense importance to Christendom, have been omitted. But though they have been important their omission here is unimportant. It was inevitable that this particular book should talk about Dante and not about Descartes, since its special themes are found much more in Dante than in Descartes. Nevertheless, I hope the curve of history has been justly followed, as I hope and believe that all the dates and details are accurate. If I have made a mistake anywhere, it is not for want of reference to the specialists, but from the mere stupidity of human nature. An effort has been made to keep proportion; the final modern chapter has not been allowed to run away with the book. A motto which might have been set on the title-page but has been, less ostentatiously, put here instead, is a phrase which I once supposed to come from Augustine, but I am informed by experts that it is not so, and otherwise I am ignorant of its source. The phrase is: " This also is Thou; neither is this Thou." As a maxim for living it is invaluable, and it—or its reversal—summarizes the history of the Christian Church.

I may perhaps be permitted to add that the themes of this book are also discussed, from different points of view, in other books of mine—in *Descent into Hell, He came down from Heaven,* and *Taliessin through Logres.* The first is fiction; the second is not; the third is poetry—whether that is or is not fiction.

The dedication of these pages is meant generally; but in particular for all those who have, in one place or another, cared to study with me " the half-read wisdom of dæmoniac images," and most especially for D.H.S.N., who nobly and happily disputed on the Nature of Love:

What make ye and what strive for? keep ye thought
Of us, or in new excellence divine
Is old forgot? and do ye count for nought
What the Greek did and what the Florentine?
We keep your memories well: O in your store
Live not our best joys treasured evermore?

C. W.

CHAPTER I

THE DEFINITION OF CHRISTENDOM

The beginning of Christendom is, strictly, at a point out of time. A metaphysical trigonometry finds it among the spiritual Secrets, at the meeting of two heavenward lines, one drawn from Bethany along the Ascent of Messias, the other from Jerusalem against the Descent of the Paraclete. That measurement, the measurement of eternity in operation, of the bright cloud and the rushing wind, is, in effect, theology.

The history of Christendom is the history of an operation. It is an operation of the Holy Ghost towards Christ, under the conditions of our humanity; and it was our humanity which gave the signal, as it were, for that operation. The visible beginning of the Church is at Pentecost, but that is only a result of its actual beginning—and ending—in heaven. In fact, all the external world, as we know it, is always a result. Our causes are concealed, and mankind becomes to us a mass of contending unrelated effects. It is the effort to relate the effects conveniently without touching, without (often) understanding, the causes that makes life difficult. The Church is, on its own showing, the exhibition and the correction of all causes. It began its career by arguing about its own cause—in such time as it had to spare from its even greater business of coming into existence.

Historically, its beginning was clear enough. There had appeared in Palestine, during the government of the Princeps Augustus and his successor Tiberius, a certain being. This being was in the form of a man, a peripatetic teacher, a thaumaturgical orator. There were plenty of the sort about, springing up in the newly-established peace of the Empire, but this particular one had a higher potential of power, and a much more distracting method. It had a very effective verbal style, notably in imprecation, together with a recurrent ambiguity of statement. It continually scored debating-points over its interlocutors. It agreed with everything on the one hand, and denounced everything on the other. For example, it said nothing against the Roman occupation : it urged obedience to the Jewish hierarchy; it proclaimed holiness to the Lord. But it was present at doubtfully holy feasts; it associated with rich men and loose women; it commented acerbly on the habits of the hierarchy; and while encouraging everyone to pay their debts, it radiated a general disapproval, or at least doubt, of every kind of property. It talked of love in terms of hell, and of hell in terms of perfection. And finally it talked at the top of its piercing voice about itself and its own unequalled importance. It said that it was the best and worst thing that ever had happened or ever could happen to man. It said it could control anything and yet had to submit to everything. It said its Father in Heaven would do anything it wished, but that for itself it would do nothing but what its Father in Heaven wished. And it promised that when it had disappeared, it would cause some other Power to illumine, confirm, and direct that small group of stupefied and helpless followers whom it deigned, with the sound of the rush of a sublime tenderness, to call its friends.

It did disappear—either by death and burial, as its opponents held, or, as its followers afterwards asserted, by some later and less usual method. Those followers at any rate remained, according to all the evidence, in a small secret group in Jerusalem. They supposed themselves to be waiting for the new manifestation which had been promised, in order that they might take up the work which their Lord had left them. According to their own evidence, the manifestation came. At a particular moment, and by no means secretly, the heavenly Secrets opened upon them, and there was communicated to that group of Jews, in a rush of wind and a dazzle of tongued flames, the secret of the Paraclete in the Church. Our Lord Messias had vanished in his flesh; our Lord the Spirit expressed himself towards the flesh and spirit of the disciples. The Church, itself one of the Secrets, began to be.

The Spirit also had his epiphany to the farther world. He had manifested before the nations—those from the parts of Libya about Cyrene, strangers of Rome, and the rest. Before ever the official missions began, the dispersed thousands who on that day had caught something of the vision and heard something of the doctrine, and had even—some of them— been convinced by vision and doctrine to submit to a Rite, to baptism, had returned to their own land, if not as missionaries yet as witnesses. The Spirit took his own means to found and to spread Christendom before a single apostolic step had left Jerusalem. It prepared the way before itself. Yet this was but a demonstration, as it were; the real work was now to begin, and the burden of the work was accepted by the group in the city. That work was the regeneration of mankind. The word has, too often, lost its force; it should be recovered. The apostles set out to generate mankind anew.

They had not the language; they had not the ideas; they had to discover everything. They had only one fact, and that was that *it had happened*. Messias had come, and been killed, and risen; and they had been dead "in trespasses and sin," and now they were *not*. They were re-generate; so might everyone be. "The promise," they called to the crowd at Jerusalem, "is to you, and to your children, and to all that are afar off." "Repent and be baptized everyone of you in the name of Jesus Christ for the remission of sins, and ye shall receive the Holy Ghost." They had believed in Jesus of Nazareth, without very clearly understanding him; his Resurrection had seemed to justify them; but much more now they were justified, or rather he was justified. The thing had happened. In every kind of way it was true that the God of Israel would not leave their souls in hell nor suffer his Holy One to see corruption.

So far the apostles. They had, in their turn, to proceed to the operation which the Spirit had begun. But the operation had to be continued under conditions; and the conditions at that moment were three—Jewish religion, Roman order, Greek intellect. Messias had been necessarily rejected and denounced on his cross in all three tongues and by all three elements—piety, government, culture. The Church, though no doubt it later came to regard itself as being, eternally, the cause of Judah and of all salvations, appeared very much at the moment as nothing but a successor to and a substitute for Judah. It proposed at first to continue a habitual consciousness of Judah. Messias himself had been a Jew; he had been put to death for blasphemy, but for Jewish blasphemy. His comments on the Gentiles during his life had been strongly Judaic; nor is it hinted that after his Resurrection they were, since he had forgiven his executioners, any less Judaic. The apostles and disciples attended the Temple. The missionaries of Pentecost were Jews. All this gave rise to two arguments, one within and one without the Church. The argument outside was with the Jews, and from the point of view of the Jews Christendom was nothing but a Jewish heresy. The dispute between orthodox Jews and heretical Jews was on one point only—had or had not the temporal mission of Judah been completed? had it been fulfilled? must Judah now abdicate? It is difficult for an individual (as is so often seen in family life) and almost impossible for an institution to abdicate in favour of its child and successor, especially in matters of philosophy. The Jews did not propose to try. They maintained the old orthodox view of the Covenant as against the new heretical view that, in the person of Jesus of Nazareth, the Covenant had undergone a violent re-formation. There was certainly a Centre party, who were overthrown as Centres usually are. Gamaliel was the first, in Christian times, to utter a maxim too often forgotten by Christians—that there is no need to be too ardent against other people on behalf of the Omnipotence. But his protest, though at first successful, afterwards failed; and the scourging of the apostles was followed by the stoning of St. Stephen. There existed for a while an active persecution of the offending sect; it was pursued to other cities, and every

effort was made to re-establish the philosophical sublimity
of Unincarnate Deity.

Within the young Church another, and similar, argument
was no less sharp. The general view among Jews outside the
Church was that Jesus of Nazareth had been primarily a
blasphemer. But the general view inside the Church was that
he had been primarily a Jew. He had particularly not waived
a single letter of the Law; he had hardly gone farther in
liberal interpretation of the Law than some of the greater
Rabbis. He had allowed that necessity might override ceremonial, but he had discouraged any light-hearted waiving of
ceremonial. The apocryphal story of his comment to the
man seen gathering sticks on the Sabbath : " O man, if thou
knowest what thou doest, blessed art thou; but if thou
knowest not, thou art cursed," seems to have expressed his
intention. " All that the Scribes and Pharisees bid you,
observe and do." It was this maxim, and others like it, to
which the more rigorous party clung. Their maxim involved
two principles : (1) that the mission of the Church was
solely to the Jews (ii) that therefore the whole Jewish ceremonial should be maintained in its fullness. It must be
admitted that they were noble souls; rejected by the Jews,
they maintained within the new society the paramount
privileged order of the Jews. And they seem, at first, to have
been the dominant party within the Church.

Yet they failed. The argument eventually was decided
against them, and decided by the agreed voices of the leaders
of the Church. The Council of Jerusalem issued its decision,
with the ratification of a phrase almost incredible in its fullness,
and yet natural in its simplicity : " It seemed good to the Holy
Ghost and to us." The sentence is, from one point of view,
absurd; from another, quite ordinary. But it is neither; it
is the serious implicit declaration by men that a union exists,
a union denied, defeated, forgotten, frustrated, but, at the
bottom of all, actual by a common consent. There are wild
moments when anyone may find himself saying—with some
truth—" It seems good to the Holy Ghost and to us." But

the Church has never forgotten, though it may apostatize often, that this is the real claim towards which it must, inevitably and indefectibly, aspire, and in which, awfully, it believes : " It seemed good to the Holy Ghost "—O vision of certainty! —" and to us "—O vision of absurdity!—. . . and what? " to lay upon you no greater burden than these necessary things." It is the choice of necessity; it is the freedom of all that is beyond necessity. But the analysis of that choice of necessity waited, and waits, for a farther vision, perhaps the understanding of the epistles of Paul.

The chief direct causes of the decision were the opinion of St. Peter, who declared that he had a vision of the proper method, the quite particular liberal intensity of St. Paul, and (at a later date) the destruction of Jerusalem. But these causes operated in support of an idea, and the idea was already latent in the controversy. The Christology of the Church already reposed in certain obscure and undeveloped formulæ. But this was a question, not so much of the nature of Christ, a phrase which might have seemed strange to the Apostolic Councils, as of the way in which that nature was to be regarded. Was the God-Man (the phrase would not have been easy to them) to be regarded as Judaic? Or was Judaism only an accident of the God-Man? Was Manhood or Judaism to come first? The Church, or the Spirit in the Church, corrected its original misconceptions, springing from the phenomena of the human nature of Messias. Grace was to be mediated universally—to Gentile as to Jew—through all the new creation. Race had nothing whatever to do with it; rites had nothing whatever to do with it. The decision has lasted universally, in spite of any sins of individual Christians or of classes of Christians at various times. No idea, no nationality, no faith, no anything, has been allowed anywhere or at any time to interpose as a primal and necessary condition of Christianity. No personal experience, however it may have preceded or led to Christianity, has been allowed to interpose between the God-Man and the soul. All doctrine, and all doctors, have been relegated into subordination.

This result was achieved very largely by the event known as the Conversion of St. Paul. It was, in every way, a very remarkable event. For first, it was the beginning of that great train of conversions and illuminations which form part of the history of Christendom—Augustine, Francis, Luther, Ignatius, Wesley, and the rest. No doubt all creeds are so accompanied; this is not the place to discuss the others. Such conversions cannot be supposed to prove the truth of a creed. Second, it turned, of course, a strong opponent of the Church into a strong supporter; but here it did more—it produced a kind of microcosm of the situation. It exploded an intense Judaizer into an anti-Judaizer. It united, as it were, Paul the Jew to Paul the man, and it gave the manhood the dominating place. But also it united Paul the man with Paul the new man, and it gave the new manhood the dominating place. It did all this in a personality which possessed, with much other genius, a desire to understand and a desire to explain. In order to understand and to explain the convert produced practically a new vocabulary. To call him a poet would be perhaps improper (besides ignoring the minor but important fact that he wrote in prose). But he used words as poets do; he regenerated them. And by St. Paul's regeneration of words he gave theology first to the Christian Church.

It was not, of course, then obvious. The Epistles were not bound up together and bought for a shilling. There must have been many of the Churches that he founded who were so illiterate as not to have heard of his best purple passages. He may have changed his mind upon certain points; he certainly took into consideration other points of view. The old silly view that he contradicted Jesus Christ on every important matter and that none of the other Apostles noticed it, or that their faint objections have faded from all record, has probably vanished along with other dim myths of the simple Gospel. The one practically certain thing about the early Church is that all the Churches, by whomever founded or taught, largely agreed. And they seem to have agreed with St. Paul about the explanation as much as he agreed with them about the fact.

The fact then had happened. The doctrine of grace was the statement of the fact; the fresh morality was the adjustment of the individual to the fact; faith was the activity that united the individual to the fact. And the fact was (among other things) that the law—the law of right living, of holiness, of love—which could not be obeyed by man had discovered a way of obeying itself in every man who chose. Man perished if he did not obey the law. Yet the law was impossible, and it could not be modified or it would become other than itself, and that could not be. What then? how was man to find existence possible? By the impossibility doing its own impossible work on man's behalf, by the forgiveness (that is, the redemption) of sins, by faith, by eternal life; past, present, future states, yet all one, and the name of that state " the love of God which is in Christ Jesus our Lord."—" The whole creation groaneth and travaileth in pain "; " God had concluded them all in unbelief that he might have mercy upon them all."

The great phrases revealed man in the bottomless hell of the corruptible in order that that corruptible might put on incorruption, that we should all be changed. " It is sown in weakness; it is raised in power." " Old things are passed away; behold, all things are become new." " God was in Christ, reconciling the world to himself . . . and hath committed unto us the word of reconciliation." " He hath made him to be sin for us, who knew no sin; that we might be made the righteousness of God in him "—" an exceeding and eternal weight of glory." In such words there was defined the new state of being, a state of redemption, of co-inherence, made actual by that divine substitution, " He in us and we in him."

It was then this apocalyptic definition which refused, for all Paul's own original godly Judaic past, to be contained either in Judaism or original godliness. Neither Judaism nor godliness could be a necessary preliminary. Certainly wherever the now multiplying missions of the Church went, they would, as a matter of courtesy, go first to the synagogue in any town they reached. It was the veil of the Jewish Temple that had been rent in twain, and was the holier for the rending. But if the Jews refused the knowledge of the fact, and indeed whether they did or not, then the missionaries turned to the Gentiles. It was not for the Jews alone that the witnesses to the Faith, to the Act, to the Happening and the Happened—were meant.

At that time, indeed, the Church seems to have moved in a cloud of wonders, as if the exact pattern of the Glory was for awhile discerned. It was not only her more formal and central Rites—Baptism and the Eucharist—which were maintained and spread and sacramentally pledged to converts. As if the Ascent of Messias had opened heaven, as if the Descent of the Paraclete had brought heaven out, the languages and habits of heaven seemed for a few years, a few decades, to hover within the Church after a manner hardly realized since except occasionally and individually. There were miracles of healing and even miracles of destruction. In that first full vision and realization, powers exchanged themselves between believers. As in other great experiences, the primal sense of this experience renewed energies more than mortal. At that time the Spirit in the Church sent " through every power a double power Beyond their functions and their offices." And this power was recognized and accepted. " After the Eucharist, certain inspired persons began to preach and to make manifest before the assembly the presence of the spirit which animated them. The prophets, the ecstatics, the speakers in tongues, the interpreters, the supernatural healers, absorbed at this time the attention of the faithful. There was, as it were, a Liturgy of the Holy Ghost after the Liturgy of Christ, a true liturgy with a Real Presence and communion. The inspiration could be felt—it sent a thrill through the organs of certain privileged persons, but the whole assembly was moved, edified, and even more or less ravished, by it and transported into the Divine sphere of the Paraclete "[1]

These things were gradually to fade. There was among them another method, also to fade, and yet of high interest and perhaps still of concern, dangerous but dangerous with a kind of heavenly daring. There grew up, it seems, in that young and ardent body an effort towards a particular spiritual experiment of, say, the polarization of the senses. Our knowledge of it is very small, and is indeed confined to a famous passage of St. Paul, to a letter of St. Cyprian's, and to one or two disapproving Canons of various Councils. The method was probably not confined to the Church; it is likely to have existed in other Mysteries. The great necromancer Simon Magus carried with him on his wanderings a companion who may have been for that purpose, and there were attributed to her high titles.

> *Thou art Helen of Tyre*
> *And hast been Helen of Troy, and hast been Rahab,*
> *The Queen of Sheba, and Semiramis,*
> *And Sara of seven husbands, and Jezebel,*
> *And other women of the like allurements,*
> *And now thou art Minerva, the first Æon,*
> *The Mother of Angels.*

But Simon is said to have preached that he had himself appeared " among the Jews as the Son, but in Samaria as the Father, and among other nations as the Holy Ghost." Christians, less ambitious, attempted the experiment both within the doctrine and within the morality of the Church. This is clear from that passage in St. Paul which shows that in some instances the experiment broke down owing to the sexual element between the man and the woman becoming too pronounced. The Apostle is asked whether, in such cases, marriage is permissible, and he answers that though, all things considered (and he meant precisely *all things considered*), it would be better if they could have continued

[1] L. Duchesne, *Christian Worship*.

with the great work, because marriage means the introduction of all sorts of pleasant—but less urgent—temporal affairs, still there is nothing wrong with it, nothing against the Faith and the New Life. If sex is becoming an inconvenience, let them deal with it in the simplest and happiest way; it is better to marry than to burn.

It seems that there was, in the first full rush of the Church, an attempt, encouraged by the Apostles, to "sublimate." But the experimenters probably did not call it that. The energy of the effort was in and towards the Crucified and Glorified Redeemer, towards a work of exchange and substitution, a union on earth and in heaven with that Love which was now understood to be capable of loving and of being loved. In some cases it failed. But we know nothing —most unfortunately—of the cases in which it did not fail, and that there were such cases seems clear from St. Paul's quite simple acceptance of the idea. By the time of Cyprian, Bishop of Carthage in the third century, the ecclesiastical authorities were much more doubtful. The women—*sub-introductæ* as they were called—apparently slept with their companions without intercourse; Cyprian does not exactly disbelieve them, but he discourages the practice.[2] And the Synod of Elvira (305) and the Council of Nicæa (325) forbade it altogether. The great experiment had to be abandoned because of "scandal."

Tolstoy put the crude objection in the *Kreutzer Sonata,* and Cyprian more or less agreed. "But then, excuse me, why do they go to bed together?" Both wise men were justified as against a great deal of sentimental lust and sensual hypocrisy. But even Cyprian and Tolstoy did not understand all the methods of the Blessed Spirit in Christendom. The prohibition was natural. Yet it seems a pity that the Church, which realized once that she was founded on a Scandal, not only to the world but to the soul, should be so nervously

[2] "We must interfere at once with such as these, that they may be separated while yet they can be separated in innocence." *The Writings of Cyprian*: *Epistle lxi*: R. E. Wallis.

alive to scandals. It was one of the earliest triumphs of "the weaker brethren," those innocent sheep who by mere volume of imbecility have trampled over many delicate and attractive flowers in Christendom. It is the loss, so early, of a tradition whose departure left the Church rather over-aware of sex, when it might have been creating a polarity with which sex is only partly coincident. The use of sex, in this experiment, might have been to pass below itself and release the dark gods of D. H. Lawrence directly into the kingdom of Messias. It failed, and it must be added that St. Paul's foresight was justified. The Church abandoned that method in favour of the marriage method, which he had deprecated, and eventually lost any really active tradition of marriage itself as a way of the soul. This we have still to recover; it is, no doubt, practised in a million homes, but it can hardly be said to have been diagrammatized or taught by the authorities. Monogamy and meekness have been taught instead.

Yet in some sense this experiment in polarization corresponded to the first knowledge of the Church; the grand experience of, and faith in, an otherness and a union, a life from others or from another. The lovers of that period—or some of them—realized the impact of Love, and desired to act and grow from it. It was the beginning, and they conceived it so. The point of its discovery was the point to be at once practised and transformed. Christianity is, always, the redemption of a point, of one particular point. "*Now* is the accepted time; *now* is the day of salvation." In this sense there is nothing but *now*; there is no duration. We have nothing to do with duration, and yet (being mortal) we have to do with nothing but duration; between those contrasts also all the history and doctrine of Christendom lies.

Immediacy and devotion, which created that lost experiment, had marked the existence and spread of the Church everywhere. The Epistles of St. Paul carry that *Now* to the highest point of exploration and of expression. But already in the Epistles themselves something else has come in. "It is!"

they said, but then they had to go on saying "It is!" Time existed, and time itself had, as it were, to be converted, to be rededicated towards the thing out of time. Not only so, but it had to be converted in the case of every individual Christian. We have often been told how the Church expected the Second Coming of Christ immediately, and no doubt this was so in the ordinary literal sense. But it was certainly expected also in another sense. The converts in all the cities of Asia and (soon) of Europe where the small groups were founded had known, in their conversion, one way or another, a first coming of their Redeemer. And then? And then! That was the consequent task and trouble—the *then*. He had come, and they adored and believed, they communicated and practised, and waited for his further exhibition of himself. The *then* lasted, and there seemed to be no farther equivalent *Now*. Time became the individual and catholic problem. The Church had to become as catholic—as universal and as durable—as time.

Time has been said to be the great problem for philosophers; nor is it otherwise with the believers. How, and with what, do we fill time? How, and how far, do we pass out of time? The apostates are only those who abandon the problem; the saints are only those who solve it. The prayer for final perseverance which the Church so urgently recommends is but her passion for remaining faithful, at least, to the problem —of refusing to give it up. What are the relations between that *Now* and the consequent *Then*? what are the conditions of the relation—not what ought to be, but what *are*? "The conversion of time by the Holy Ghost" is the title of the grand activity of the Church.

In the first century, in the Apostolic age itself, that time which the Church was to redeem was already becoming the bane of the Church. The first division between the Church and what has been called the Kingdom began to exist. The Kingdom—or, apocalyptically, the City—is the state into which Christendom is called; but, except in vision, she is not yet the City. The City is the state which the Church is to become. In the impact of Messias, in the evocation of her elements, in the impact of the Spirit, in the promulgation of her unity, she for a moment, was one with her state. But she was too soon all but divided from her state. It was inevitable; had it not been so, she would have had no reason for existing. Her reason is not only in the error of the world; it is in her own error. Her error is her very opportunity for being. That is what she is about.

Time then existed, and she reconciled herself to it. The Jewish problem had been settled. But the other conditions, the Roman organization, the Greek culture, remained. Neither of them were—to use a favourite political phrase—" opposed in principle " to the Christian idea. " Scores of dim sects were struggling for existence among the lower classes "[8] and, one might add, among the upper. In a general way, the Roman Government entirely approved of its citizens and subjects preoccupying themselves with their private religious fancies. The Government's own business was to keep their world fed, to keep their world quiet, and to keep their world " hilarious." (It was *Hilaritas Populi Romani* on which, at a later period, the coins of Hadrian, as it were, congratulated the Emperor.) They had, for that reason, at a later period, to concentrate formal attention on the person and providence of the Emperor. But people were not sacrificing to the Emperor all the time, and in other rituals the Governments were not interested. St. Paul travelled in an Empire of which he approved, and which, largely, approved of him. He had the highest respect for the magistrates, and they had little fault to find with him. He had some odd deity, but that was common enough. Salvation, initiation, second birth, were ordinary dinner-talk and public-house chat. Nicodemus may have found difficulties in the idea, but no ordinary person in the non-Judaic world would have blenched. Pilate had been quite unmoved—except to a mild curiosity—by assertions that Jesus had called himself the Son of God; he was only a little surprised that the Jews

[8] *Origins of Christianity,* Charles Bigg.

should resent it. Christianity, so far as anyone understood it, was naturally supposed to be a tolerant religion, as tolerant as any of its rivals; its credal intolerance was as shocking then, when discovered, as it is to-day. The Jewish objections had involved the Apostles in dangers, but the final decision of the Government at Rome in St. Paul's own case seems to have allowed that Christianity was a permissible creed. It was roughly regarded as a variation of Judaism.

The break in this more or less agreeable unity was due directly to Nero; how exactly he was influenced we do not know. The Great Fire of Rome broke out in July A.D. 64. The natural tendency to blame someone unpopular caused rumours that the Emperor himself was responsible, much as the Roman Catholics were blamed for the Great Fire of London in 1666. The Emperor and the Government transferred the blame to the Christians, and the statement was accepted. The Christians were accused not only of the definite act but of the more general evil of " a hatred of mankind." Notable intellectuals like Tacitus accepted the notion. Tacitus, it has been said, was " a Stoic noble who hated Nero and hated the Christians and could not decide which he hated most." One would have supposed that this first outbreak of persecution would have caused all later Christians to have hesitated over belief in popular rumour, official assurances, and partisan histories. It has not done so. The blazing crosses of the Vatican gardens throw their lurid light on all our easy credulity, on the *I heards* and *he saids* of our daily life; our repetitions bark like the dogs to whom the faithful, wrapped in wild beasts' skins, were thrown. Christianity became suspect and remained suspect. It was regarded with horror by many and with aversion by most. There was, however, some reason for the aversion (apart from the necessary spiritual scandal and from the fact that the Christians —or one of them—replied to the persecution with that admirable but extreme revolutionary pamphlet called *The Revelation of St. John the Divine*).

This suspicion obviously existed in different degrees at

different times and in different places. Its effect was entirely incalculable. It depended on the feeling of the crowd, the temper of the magistrates, the progress of public affairs, the predilections of the Emperor, and a score of other chances. It depended also on the temperament and behaviour of the Christians. The more converts, the more variations in relation with their philosophical or religious neighbours. There were (as time went on) timid and tempestuous Christians, Christians who were delicate and quiet, and Christians who were disputatious and querulous. The main difference, indeed, was official and social, and even more social than official. The web of that vast Empire hummed steadily to the formal " adoration " of the Genius of the Emperor. But on the other hand no adoration could be less like anything meant by religious adoration than that. It was, no doubt, a more formal thing than our own genuflexions to the Throne, but then it would be treated also as more absurd. " I think I am about to become a god," said the dying Vespasian ; it was embarrassing to everyone when the Christians solemnly and formally anathematized what no one had ever dreamt of believing. It is bad enough to be contradicted on what one does believe ; it is intolerable to be contradicted—perhaps with vehemence or superiority—on what one obviously does not believe. The Jews, it is true, did not adore ; but everyone knew about the Jews. They were formally excused ; they were a racial, not a religious, body, or only religious because racial ; and they were not at all propagandist. It was extremely difficult to become a Jew. But it was becoming more and more difficult not to be harried by suggestions that one ought to become a Christian. The Church was attacking on all sides and in all manners—by persuasion, by argument, almost by threats. Its purpose, of which it made no secret, was to evangelize the world. In the eyes of most of the Empire, this meant primarily a separation from official activities, from social holidays, from festivities and games, from anything that involved the worship of the Genius of the Emperor and the admission that other deities might exist or other mysteries be illuminating. The quietest and nicest Christians tactfully stopped away on such occasions; if they came they did not inquire about "meats offered to idols"; they did not parade their consciences. But since they did not, in the last resort, wish to pour our libations to the household gods of their friends, they were all driven gradually—or suddenly—to drop dinner-parties. To any ordinary Roman it was all very odd and rather beastly.

With the growth of the Christian numbers the oddness and the beastliness became more marked. The Government became more and more conscious of this minority of dissidents. The position was rather like our own international position; war might break out at any time, but for surprisingly long periods it did not. Domitian, frightened by a conspiracy, struck at the Christians near his person. Pliny, as Governor of Bithynia, found Christians denounced to him. He tortured a few to discover what, in fact, they believed, and wrote to Trajan. Trajan took the proper Imperial view. Christians were not to be hunted down; informations against them were not to be encouraged, and if the informer were found to be merely untruthful, he was to be punished. It was not, normally, the habit of the Government to encourage the delation of one set of citizens by others. But, on the same principle of encouraging a quiet life everywhere, if the delation were found to be justified, if so-and-so really did stand out against the public security, the public good, he must be dealt with as a criminal. He was, of course, a criminal. Christians regarded themselves as sinners, and other people regarded them as criminals.

It was probably the need for formal denunciation that explains "the brethren" visiting confessors in custody, quite apart from the obvious bribery of guards that went on. The journey of Ignatius from Antioch to Rome is the great example. A Christian under arrest, unless in a time of severe persecution, was a man guilty of a particular crime. It did not follow that his visitors were guilty of that crime. No doubt a certain risk was run; but no doubt also some Christians might be visited by pagan friends who, if sacrifice were demanded, would sacrifice. Any common informer against them might find himself in trouble. Hadrian even insisted that the " delator " must specify some mis-behaviour besides Christianity. But in general Christianity was enough to justify examination, and examination meant death.

On the other hand, Christians were not attacked on religious grounds, and were in some ways even protected. Their burial places remained undisturbed, guarded by all the severe care of the Roman law for sepulchres. Cemeteries belonged to the *Dei Manes,* the gods of the underworld, and the mercy which the Genius of the Emperor refused in the light of the Roman day, the dark divinities beyond the tomb retained, as if in an awful recognition of the God who had gone among them and returned. The catacombs have been preserved to us by that care, and by the careful legalism of the Roman Pontiffs who watched the propriety of the dead. Nor apparently were churches, when at last they came to be built, usually attacked. The Roman law was very careful of property. There may have been a little underhand legal work in the matter of forming guilds to own the churches, but there they were and there they stopped. The old pictures in which Roman soldiers broke in to seize the worshippers by the altar are defined by the admirable phrase : " My dear, you exaggerate." " Those who have died for the Christian faith ", said Origen, " at different times have been few and are easily counted." He spoke relatively, no doubt, but he meant something like it. Delation, mob riots, but little inter-ference by the official rulers of Rome. It was not until the beginning of the third century that Tertullian could cry out : " *Non licet esse nos* "—" it is not allowed to us to exist." Virgil and Peter then were at odds in the streets of Rome.

Such was the exterior position, through the first two centuries, of developing Christendom—uncertain, often diffi-cult, sometimes fatal, but often tolerable, and even some-times easy. Meanwhile Christendom had begun to under-stand itself—or at least to understand a little of itself. The grand discovery made by the Church, expressed by St. Paul, and promulgated with intense enthusiasm, had only begun to define, in the most general way, its own nature. " Remembering *how* she felt but *what* she felt Remembering not "— or rather not exactly knowing, the infant Church pursued its way, a very little distance down the ages. That happened to it which happens to all such tremendous experiences. The Romantic discovery was followed by a grand intellectual Romantic movement, as it might be called. It was inevitable; it was proper. But it went, as Romanticism unchecked will, to the wildest extremes. It was almost a literary movement; in the days of printing it would have been a literary movement. It had two sections, the one harmless if unreliable, the second harmful and even less reliable. The first consisted of the romantic tales of Christ and the Apostles. There were accounts of the Childhood, and how the Lord at a tender age blasted his schoolmaster with a withered arm, or, even more fiercely, slew his uncivil boyish companion (and healed him after). There were stories of the Blessed Virgin, and what happened to the High Priest when he interfered with her funeral. There were more or less credible tales of the Apostles and the visions of the Apostles. There was as yet no Canon of Documents accepted by the Church as inspired, and these floated round with the more authentic writings. Some edified and some did not, but they did not much relate to serious matters.

The other part of this Romantic movement was much more deadly. It was a more philosophical Romanticism, or rather it was a Romanticism which expressed itself in terms of philosophy. Of the writings of this kind it has been said that they were those " which in larger or smaller circles were placed on a level with those of our Canon, but were regarded by the Church at large as the Book of Mormon or the writings of Mrs. Eddy are now."[4] They developed, and the teachers who were related to them developed, the usual marks of the lost Romantic. The lost or pseudo-Romantic, in all times

[4] *Apocryphal New Testament,* M. R. James.

and places, has the same marks, and he had them in the
early centuries of the Faith. He was then called a Gnostic.
The Gnostic schools were many. They sprang from the con-
tact of the Faith with the less reputable Greek metaphysics
and the wilder Near-Eastern inventions. But they all tended
to develop along the same lines. They accepted the idea of
Salvation; they accepted heavenly beings in operation; they
accepted supreme and passionless Deity. They then proceeded
to purify these ideas from the low and crude interpretations
which a materialistic Christianity had somehow introduced
into them. They did this, mostly, in three ways.

(1) They removed from that supreme Godhead of theirs
any tendency to creation, especially any tendency to the
creation of matter, and most especially any tendency to
the creation of anything capable of " evil." They regarded
creation in a Deity not so much as impossible as indecent.
But they allowed to It certain emanations or supernatural
outputtings, and to those yet others, and to those yet others
again, until they had imagined " a long chain of divine
creatures, each weaker than its parent," and came at last
" to one who, while powerful enough to create is silly enough
not to see the creation is wrong."[5] This was the God of this
world.

(2) The exact relationships of the spiral of emanations
differed in the different schools. But they agreed that somehow the pure light of the lower heaven had got involved in
this unpleasant business of matter and had to be redeemed.
It was set free by the descent of a Redemption which, however, itself put on merely the appearance of matter and withdrew it long before the Passion and Crucifixion could in any
way stain its own lordly spirituality. At the Baptism, or thereabouts, the Divinity descended into the man Jesus of Nazareth;
at the Arrest, or thereabouts, it withdrew. What was scourged
and slain was not it. In some cases it was Jesus the man;
but more fantastic inventions—not unattractive—were offered.
The Gospel of Barnabas, for example (however late), re-

[5] *Origins of Christianity,* Charles Bigg.

counted how the Lord had changed Judas Iscariot into an appearance of himself, so that the guard in confusion seized Judas, and finally in the same error crucified him; while the Lord from heaven surveyed his discreet vengeance.[6]

(3) There began to be drawn a definite division among Gnostic believers. There were the lower spiritual classes—the proletariat and bourgeoisie of heaven—who lived by faith. There were the upper spirtual classes who lived by knowledge; the illuminated, the perfect. No doubt the illuminated began low down in the scale, but they speedily rose; they saw. As if in an early parallel to our modern educational system, they passed by a series of scholarships of enlightenment from Council School to Secondary School and to University. Others, " not so blest as they," remained in the classes where they had been spiritually born. Like Mr. E. M. Forster's business man in a wood, they stared at the hierarchies of glory and could not see them. They were not capable of the *Gnosis,* of the Mystery.

All these views were fervently rejected by the general opinion of the Church. The revolt against the Gnostic influence depended on two things. There was the capacity of individual anti-Gnostic writers, such as Irenæus of Lyons. There was also—and far more important—the actual belief of the separate Churches. It was on many points yet undefined; there were speculative points on which it has not yet been defined. But all those groups in all those cities, founded in the apostolic doctrine, made it clear that they did not, in fact, believe what the Romantic philosophers declared; that this was not the Faith as they had received and held it. What did the Churches believe? They believed that Almighty God—the final Deity—had Itself created heaven and earth, and was, as the First and Only Cause of them, finally responsible for them. They believed that Jesus Christ was the Son of the Father—in that Deity—and had been materially born on earth *ex Maria Virgine.* They believed, that is, that the

[6] Assuming, as is suggested, that the present 16th-century text derived from the lost Gnostic Gospel which once existed.

First and Only Cause initiated, operated, and concluded Redemption. They rejected, with great energy, the idea that cause belonged to a subordinate Demiurgus and the idea that there was a special kind of superior redemption for superior persons. No doubt there were prophets and speakers with tongues and teachers and so on; no doubt Almighty God operated peculiarly through certain individuals. But they repudiated any opposition between faith and vision. Faith was not a poor substitute for vision; it was rather the capacity for integrating the whole being with truth. It was a total disposition and a total act. By definition, all men were in need of salvation; therefore, of faith and repentance in faith. The Gnostic view left little room for the *illuminati* to practise love on this earth; "they live as though they were indifferent," said Irenæus. The Church anathematized the pseudo-Romantic heresies; there could be no superiority except in morals, in labour, in love. *See, understand, enjoy,* said the Gnostic; *repent, believe, love,* said the Church, *and if you see anything by the way, say so.*

In some sense, the Gnostics avoided any "scandal" to the mind and soul. The stones they offered fitted the corners of many temples; only not of the City of Christendom. God was not really responsible for the appalling putrescence of misery which we call the world. The soul and the body (so to divide them formally) were not responsible for each other. Men were not responsible for each other. The Gordian knot of the unity was cut, and the bits fell radically apart. Toothache, cancer, women's periods, frustrated sex-love, these and other ills were without relation to the activity of the celestial spheres. "In the fifteenth year of Tiberius Cæsar the Christ came down from heaven," wrote Marcion, one of the last and one of the greatest of the Gnostics, but the orthodox answer was that, years earlier, he had been generated on earth: "the book of the generations of Jesus Christ."

Meanwhile the general consent of the Church was producing a written orthodoxy, "of whose authority," to quote the Articles of the Church of England, "was never any doubt in the Church." Never is a long time. But it is true that the Canon of the New Testament emerges about this time, not by dogmatic decisions but by a common assent, out of the growing mass of Christian writing. This, in fact, is its only ratification. Why the New Testament? because Christendom universally produced it. But why Christendom? Roughly, because if Christendom is what it says it is—for example, in the New Testament—then it is a Nature in which we choose to believe, as against the personal righteousness, the social order, the cultural speculation. By the end of the second century, the New Testament was all but complete and was certainly authoritative; by the same period, Christendom was organized, and the grand battle was about to open.

CHAPTER II

THE RECONCILIATION WITH TIME

From the middle of the second century five names stand out—Montanus, Marcus Aurelius, Tertullian, Clement, and Origen. Together they prefigure a kind of reconciliation between the Church and the ordinary process of things, even though in one instance that prefiguring takes the shape of a more violent conflict. It would not be true to say that the Church consented to have her extraordinary supernatural graces driven underground; it would be truer to say that she made preparations for drawing into herself the whole of normal human existence. A change of method, an assent already in operation, became more marked. She suffered, she manipulated, she hierarchized, she intellectualized. All this she had done already, but now she entered upon it as a steady mode of behaviour.

In one instance the prefigured reconciliation took its opposite shape. In the year 161 Marcus Aurelius Antoninus ascended the Julian throne. Under that strenuous and ethical rationalist, persecution began to change. The self-consciousness of the Empire as regards Christians took, through the mind and person of the Emperor, a more deliberate form. What had been irritation, fury, riots of the blood, became a deliberate moral and intellectual effort. The pressure of Christendom on Rome had become too great. The Empire determined to shake itself free from this troublesome delirium of its mind, this haunting disease of its body. The effort was deliberate and prolonged. " The persecutions under Marcus Aurelius extend throughout his reign. They were fierce and deliberate. . . . They had the Emperor's direct personal sanction. They break out in all parts of the Empire: in Rome, in Asia Minor, in Gaul, in Africa; possibly also

in Byzantium."[1] The " good " Emperors had come to regard
Christianity as an evil, as all tolerant and noble non-Christian
minds tend to do. Partly, no doubt, the best Emperors had
the highest idea of their duty to the safety of the State. But
also they had the highest sense of moral balance and the least
sense of the necessity of Redemption. The worse Emperors
—Commodus, Heliogabalus—had a more superstitious impulse which was certainly more in accord with the asserted
dogmas of the Gospel. Gods, and the nature of the Gods,
are likely to be better understood by sinful than by stoical
minds.

In Asia Polycarp, in Rome Justin Martyr, in Gaul Irenæus,
and many more perished. With the names of such men
is registered under Severus the name of a slave who not
only endured martyrdom but in a sentence defined the
Faith. Her name was Felicitas; she was Carthaginian; she
lay in prison; there she bore a child. In her pain she screamed.
The jailers asked her how, if she shrieked at *that,* she expected
to endure death by the beasts. She said: " Now *I* suffer
what *I* suffer; then another will be in me who will suffer for
me, as I shall suffer for him." In that, Felicitas took her place
for ever among the great African doctors of the Universal
Church.

Against that persecution, as against those that followed,
the Church opposed that supernatural loyalty. But it opposed
also the protestation of a profound natural loyalty. It not
only allowed the Empire; it took refuge in the Empire; it
felt the Empire as a protection even while it feared it as a peril.
This had been so, in some sense, from the beginning. Rome
had not only held off the Germans; it had postponed Antichrist. " The mystery of iniquity doth already work; only
he who now letteth will let until he be taken out of the way.
And then that shall that Wicked One be revealed." God,
was thus in Rome itself, in the existence and order of Rome.
While this world lasted, and in proportion as time became
more and more a necessity of the Christian life, public order,

[1] Lightfoot: quoted by B. J. Kidd, *History of the Church.*

the Republic, became of almost equivalent value. Just after the Aurelian persecution had failed and faded under the ignoble Commodus, Tertullian proclaimed again the value of that temporal salvation. In his *Book of Apology Against the Heathen* he declared that Christians, far from being suppressed, were everywhere. " Men say that the State is beset by them, that Christians are in their fields, their fortresses, their islands. They murmur that each sex, each age, every consideration and every rank is going over to this sect." He protested that the Lords of the Empire made no true examination of it; no, " you harshly pass sentence : The law forbids you to exist!"

Yet he (he said), with nearly all Christians, desired to live in the sanctity of Rome. " The end of time itself, threatening terrible and grievous things, is delayed because of the time allowed to the Roman Empire." " That which God hath willed is in the Emperors, and therefore we would have that which God hath willed kept secure." He protested that Christians though they might not pray to the Genius of the Emperor, might, should, and did pray for his " good health." Many non-Christian Romans, some Emperors, and probably Marcus Aurelius himself, thought definitely that the good health of the Emperor was much more important than his Genius or his attributed Deity. Between the two moderate views there was much agreement. But their division was final. The Church, organizing itself for that process in time, had accepted the view that its members, like itself, would always have to live their lives on the basis of " faith." And the very condition of that faith was that Deity was single, supreme, and *different*. Without difference there was no Reconciliation. And Reconciliation was the supreme aim of faith.

Two things followed—perhaps inevitably followed—from that organization for process. The first was the disappearance of the extraordinary supernatural impulses. It may be that our Lord the Spirit discontinued them; one is almost driven to that view on observing how the Church discouraged them.

The very nature of the Church involves the view that, apart from human sin, what happened was right. This certainly gives a great advantage in argument to any hostile, intelligent, and sceptical mind, but the belief can hardly be abandoned because of that intellectual inconvenience. Messias seems to have indicated that in the Church, as well as in daily life, the Blessed One will conform his actions—at least, to a degree—to the decisions of his creatures. If the Church determined on something, then that something should have been or should be true; and it is arguable that Messias was born of a pure Virgin as much because the Church would believe it as for any other reason—all things else being therefore made conformable. At any rate the prophecies and the liturgies of the Spirit began to disappear.

There was one rally. It took place about the same time as the Aurelian persecution, beginning in Phrygia and spreading. It was known as the Montanist heresy, after its founder Montanus. And it is the first and last of such revolts against the habits of the Universal Church. It was the last because it was still definitely related to the actual life of the young Church; it was not an effort to return to something that had been lost for centuries. It was the last also in the sense that it was still privileged to encourage central doctrines in the Church. It was the first in the sense that it is followed by other movements, at later times, which attempted a similar austerity and a similar freedom. One might almost say that the defeat of Montanism exhibits the Church as an Institution more clearly than any other moment, and an Institution committed to reconciliation (not compromise) with ordinary men.

Montanism was, first of all, a highly rigorist movement. In morals, as in everything, there are two opposite tendencies. The first is to say: " Everything matters infinitely." The second is to say: " No doubt that is true. But mere sanity demands that we should not treat everything as mattering all that. Distinction is necessary; more-and-less is necessary; indifference is necessary." The contention is always sharp.

The Rigorous view is vital to sanctity; the Relaxed view is vital to sanity. Their union is not impossible, but it is difficult; for whichever is in power begins, after the first five minutes, to maintain itself from bad and unworthy motives. Harshness, pride, resentment encourage the one; indulgence, falsity, detestable good-fellowship the other.

Between the two good (and evil) things the idea of what the Articles of the Church of England call "works of supererogation" had already emerged. "If thou do any good thing outside the commandments of God thou shalt win for thyself more exceeding glory," wrote Hermas. It is a difficult and dangerous proposition—not made easier by the rather violent language of winning glory for oneself in which Hermas indulged. Yet the idea has lingered in the Church, and been half-formulated in the talk of the Way of the Commandments and the Way of the Counsels. The Christian doctrine has been that the demanded surrender to God must be entire, in which case there could hardly be anything supererogatory. Yet it has also been universally felt that there were, so to speak, acts of love and devotion which were not absolutely required. How can absolute surrender leave non-absolute potentialities? The answer seems largely to have lain in the doctrine of Vocation. Some were called to a strictness, some to a laxity. It naturally happened that strictness, being more difficult, was regarded as superior. So, as far as difficulty is concerned, it is; but so, as far as vocation is concerned, it is not. Relaxation is no less holy and proper than rigour, though perhaps it can hardly be preached so. But the lovely refreshments of this world in some may not be without their part in the lordly rigours of the others; the exchanges of Christendom are very deep; if we thrive by the force of the saints, they too may feed on our felicities. The life of the Redeemer is at the root of all; it is all within the Church, and (said the same Hermas, in a nobler style) "she was created before all things and for her sake the world was framed."

To us the most relaxed morals of the Church of the second

century are austere enough. But to the Montanists the
faithful seemed to have fallen away almost damnably from
their duty. They proposed to revive original decency—much
fasting, no second marriages, no kind of relation to the
State (as, for example, in education). They took the sternest
attitude towards sins committed after baptism. They refused
to allow that any of the faithful might escape from persecution.
They said, in effect, to the Church about ordinary life :
" Come out of her, my people." They denounced the normal
life of Christians at the time as sacrilegious, profane, and
idolatrous. The normal Christians with less cause and as
much heat retaliated. They even, to justify themselves,
invented romantic details against the Montanists—such as
child-murder and a cannibal Eucharist. The normal calumnies
of piety flew to and fro, encouraged by two other differences
in stress.

The first concerned the Prophets. The direct inspiration
of the Spirit had, as usual, given rise to abuses. The oracles
were paid for, a thing harmless enough in itself, since money
also is a medium of exchange, but perilous. Priests might
be, though in fact they usually were not, paid; they had
their appointed job. But it was of the essence of the prophetic
ministry that contract could not exist, nor control; the
Spirit acted *proprio motu.* Contract and control belonged to
the early developed hieratic ministry of the Church. There,
indeed, in the whole business of the sacraments which began
when the Church began, the Lord deigned to commit himself to the hands of men, and to fulfil his agreement at their
demand. The prophet at the end of the first century remained
only " here and there, a much venerated but solitary per-
sonage."

His office, in fact, had changed. The Prophecy had once
been " a Voice conveying an immediate revelation; to Polycarp, as to Origen, it is an interpretativ epower, which dis-
covers beneath the literal sense of Scripture mysteries which
are not visible to the eye of mere common sense." It had
moved from the meeting house to the study, though there it

still had disciples. Something was, no doubt, lost; something gained. But there it is; in general it had moved. The Montanists proposed to bring it back. They were orthodox; they kept the sacerdotal system—the Orders and the Formulæ. But they proposed to " enliven " these (no doubt, even then, with some cause) by subordinating them to the prophetic office and the inspired utterance. They even went further; they developed a grand principle. They were orthodox on the Nature of Christ; they were said to have been the first to use the word *homo-ousion, of the same nature,* presently to be of such import to the Church. But they possessed a special devotion to the Person of that Spirit by whom the prophets spoke. They asserted that his special age and dispensation had already begun. They are said to have been the first to call him God; if so, he permitted himself to be named in schism and defined by an error. They declared that he exhibited his moral scrupulousness by their conduct and his will by their prophets. On the general wrangle the Montanists were defeated; the prophets disappeared; morality was eased. The Universal Church secured a tenderness for men and preserved the contract with God. But it must be admitted that the Holy Spirit remained God.

Thus while on the one hand the Church declared the loyalty and claimed the protection of citizenship, on the other it organized itself into a regular and reliable method. It refused (if the phrase may be allowed) the irresponsible outbreaks and the moral extremism of the Holy Ghost for the established formulæ and the moral discipline of Messias. It had already established that system of Penance which is the only system of judgment ending, and meant to end, only in forgiveness. Sins were not to be forgotten; they were to be remembered. In those parts of Christendom where sacramental confession is not practised, the practice of confession to God has yet been retained. The fault, the failing, is to be offered to God: grace demands that everything should be recollected by man, as to God everything is present.

Man and God together can know all joyously; man without God. . . .

But there was another adjustment to be made, that of the intellect. It was not altogether easy for the Church, once she had defeated Gnosticism, to resolve on her attitude towards philosophy. Through her dioceses, among all her doctors, it was common ground that philosophy was negligible compared to the Gospel. But, that admitted, was philosophy as a study to be regarded with generosity or with reprobation? Ought a Christian to understand and speak its language? Great voices directed the Church in different ways. About the year 200 the opposite views were formulated in Africa. The vigorous rhetoric of Tertullian (soon to become a Montanist) proclaimed from Carthage the austere rejection of this world's intelligence. " Philosophy," he wrote, " is the theme of worldly wisdom, that rash interpreter of the Divine Nature and Order. And indeed the heresies are equipped by philosophy." He proceeded to run through a few Gnostic examples. Valentinus, a Platonist! Marcion, a Stoic! The Epicureans, Zeno, Heraclitus—philosophers and heretics spend their time asking whence evil came, and why; whence man came and how; and even (as Valentinus, it seemed, had done) whence came God. " Wretched Aristotle, who gave them the art of dialectic!"

He was answered by a more dulcet voice from another African city. Alexandria, the haunt of all philosophies, had nurtured also the Catholic. There among the many schools rose the Catechetical School of the Christians. Founded (it was improbably said) by St. Mark, and intended originally, as such schools everywhere were, for the instruction of believers before baptism, it grew now into the dialectic of high and subtle speculation. The educated, as well as the uneducated, were to be convinced; nor need they reject their education and refuse their capacities to the intellect of the Faith. Since Athens there had hardly been such discussions as in Alexandria, and now Alexandria had more to discuss than Athens. Since Alexandria there has hardly been such freedom of intellectual talk until to-day, and though our freedom is as great our intellect is no greater.

"Philosophy," wrote Clement of Alexandria, "becomes conducive to piety; being a kind of preparatory training to those who attain to faith through demonstration. Perhaps philosophy was given to the Greeks directly and primarily till the Lord should call the Greeks." Philosophy, he thought, was a way of preparation for the man who was to enter into "the perfection of Christ." He did not hesitate to think and speak of the *gnosis,* the knowledge. His own teacher had "engendered in the souls of his hearers a deathless element of knowledge." "There seems to me," he wrote, "to be a first kind of saving change from heathenism to faith, a second from faith to knowledge." But was there no distinction between the philosopher-Gnostic and the Christian-Gnostic? Yes surely, though Tertullian might think it insufficient. It was "the exercise of beneficence," "the love of God." Knowledge "as it passes on into love, begins at once to establish a mutual friendship between that which knows and that which is known"; he who reaches this becomes "a light standing and abiding for ever." It is perhaps worth remarking that here already are defined the stages of what came to be called the mystical Way : of Purgation, of Illumination, of Union. The first change is in belief; the second in discovery. The sweetness of Clement, brooding on pure Love, does not hide the nature of the heavenly order. "For the sake of each of us he laid down his life—worth no less than the universe. He demands of us in return our lives for the sake of each other." This is love; it is this which is to be discovered; in the most luminous knowledge of this souls exist. Another voice than Tetullian's had laid down more simply, in Carthage, the great fundament : "Another will be in me who will suffer for me as I shall suffer for him." The two African cities proclaimed the universal web of exchange, and if the slave-girl's cry is more piercing than the philosopher's doctrine, yet it was to Clement that we owe

the beginning of that philosophic thought which hinders, if
it cannot by itself prevent, apostasy.

The vocabulary of Paul and the vocabulary of the Fourth
Gospel were here united. The movement which began with
Clement and culminated later in Athanasius preserved humanism for the Church. But the immediate successor of Clement,
to deliver lectures in the School and to talk with his students
in his house, was a greater than Clement, though perhaps
a lesser than Athanasius; it was Origen. Origen has always
been suspect. He has been condemned and denounced.

    Yet constantly the opinion hath prevailed

    In the Church (that Origen) was a holy man—

and not only holy but wise, and not only wise but correct.
He has been suspected of a great orthodoxy, for the Church
has not always been most comfortable with the most orthodox.

He continued the tradition and work of Clement. It
would be improper—but not so improper—to say that the
mark of the Alexandrian school was that they were all gentlemen. One must not deny the title to other saints and doctors.
Yet there is about them a sense of the *naturalness* of Christianity, as distinguished from its catastrophic supernatural-
ness. Clement insisted on repentance and morality; and
Origen, in his heretical self-mutilation, carried morality to a
morbid and immoral extreme. But their work is, as it were,
without the macabre, the terrible, the smell of corruption.
Clement loved philosophy, and Origen laboured at scholarship. He compiled the first Polyglot Old Testament, of six
texts. He was a great commentator, a prophet (in the new
sense), a great literary critic (in the noblest sense) according
to his own time. He was the first to develop the allegorical
method of Biblical criticism; the method by which the sense,
meaning one thing literally, meant another morally or mystically or analogically. It depends, for its value, on an illumination of greatness; these meanings must be self-evident once
they are pointed out, for they cannot be proved. Like prayer,
their real aim is the interior conviction. As we contemplate
the images of the poets, so the allegorizers studied the texts

of Scripture. It is obvious that this is the most valuable, perhaps the only valuable, method with much of the text of the Bible. But it is obvious also that it lends itself to the wildest vagaries, as with, say, the Adamites, those simple believers in nature who supposed that by returning to nakedness (as in Eden) we should return to innocence (as in Eden), and vice versa. Origen, like all intelligent readers then as now, realized that he needed a check upon his own brain and he found it, where all Christians have found it, in the universal decisions of the Church. This authority he recognized; this relationship he desired. The recognition of authority is the desire for union, but also it is the knowledge that the individual by himself is bound to be wrong. The "State" of the Church was the "State" of a City. Schism was the worst sin, for schism was bound to nullify the justice from which it might arise. However right a man's ideas, they were bound to go wrong if he nourished them by himself. The value of dogma, besides its record of fact, is the opportunity it gives for the single mind to enter the Communion of Saints —say, of Intelligences. The personal thought is vitalized by that and aspires towards that. "He ceases," wrote Clement, "to be a man of God and faithful to the Lord who sets on one side the tradition of the Church."

But Origen did something more than insist on a proper obedience to authority on earth; he discovered a central obedience in the secrets of heaven. Less than fifty years after his death there were born in Africa two great opponents, Arius and Athanasius. The followers of both claimed Origen as their own doctor. This curious double claim arose from an illumination which has perhaps in itself a slightly different value. The doctrine of the Trinity had been, by Origen's day, more or less established. The Father was Creator of all; the Son was God and Man; the Holy Ghost was—the Holy Ghost. Origen held to this; he said of the Divine Son: "*Non est quando non fuerit*"—"there is not when he was not"—never have two tenses so sublimely illuminated glory. But he did more. He strongly maintained, if indeed he did not discover, the voluntary Subordination of the Son; he contemplated in Deity Itself the joy of obedience: obedience which is a particular means of joy and the only means of that particular joy. The Son is co-equal with the Father (as Origen held, and as was afterwards defined), yet the Son is obedient to the Father. A thing so sweetly known in many relations of human love is, beyond imagination, present in the midmost secrets of heaven. For the Son in his eternal Now desires subordination, and it is his. He wills to be so; he co-inheres obediently and filially in the Father, as the Father authoritatively and paternally co-inheres in him. And the whole Three Persons are co-eternal together—and co-equal. The Arians later denied it, but in the last struggle Athanasius and the representatives of humane culture won. It is true that the opposition is still maintained by the Unitarian bodies to-day—that deny love to God except by means of his creation. But the Church has not believed that there lack in Him any of love's experiences (analogically understood): of all Love's holiest loves, *non est quando non fuerit.*

The imaginations of the Alexandrian Fathers were courteous; their visions were humane. Origen extended that vision so far as to teach the final restitution of all things, including the devils themselves. It is impossible that some such dream should not linger in any courteous mind, but to teach it as a doctrine almost always ends in the denial of free-will. If God has character, if man has choice, an everlasting rejection of God by man must be admitted as a possibility; that is, hell must remain. The situation of the devils (if any) is not man's business. The charity of Origen schematized then too far; he declared as a doctrine what can only remain as a desire. It was one of the reasons why he was denounced; that and, among other things, a kind of Docetism—a fading of the flesh. He was not Manichæan, but in his high speculations the necessities of matter trembled into non-existence; he speaks somewhere of Our Lord's body being phenomenally different to each observer. On the other hand " he was the first of Christian thinkers to speak at large of the human soul in Christ, and the first to describe the union by the compound word God-Man."[2]

He had grown up under the shadow of the persecution of Septimus Severus at the beginning of the third century: nearly fifty years afterwards he was tortured in the persecution of Decius, and died from the results. That century maintained, with quiet periods, the effort of Marcus Aurelius. Decius himself is reported to have said that he would rather have a second Emperor by his side than a bishop in Rome. Under Septimus, under Decius, under Gallus and Valerian, under Aurelias, edicts were put forth against the faithful. It had been possible for Origen to say in his time that the number of those put to death for their belief, from the beginning, had not been great; it was, after his time, no longer possible.

There were certainly efforts at compromise. Heliogabalus was willing to include Christianity in his general scheme of the Mysteries, with the Sun-God and with the Palladium; and the more ethical Alexander set up a statue of Christ in his oratory beside Virgil, Orpheus, and Abraham—he even preferred that a disputed property in land should be given to the Christian society rather than to a guild of cooks. He thought that it was better for God to be worshipped " after whatever manner."

The persecutions set up other minor problems, and the relations of the Church to what may be called common sense grew more marked. The incarnation of that common sense was Cyprian, also of Carthage; he who discouraged the *subintroductæ*. Three points may be briefly mentioned—the question of flight, the question of the lapsed, and the matter of the confessors.

(i) The Montanists, and others, held that flight and secrecy were impermissible. Wild enthusiasms for martyrdom broke out. Christians hurled themselves at tribunals, demanding death. But the Mind of Christendom discouraged it. " We

2 *History of the Church*, B. J. Kidd.

have no admiration for those who denounce themselves,"
wrote the Church in Smyrna to the Church in Philomelium;
" not so does the Gospel teach us." Enthusiasm itself must
be purified; one had no right to involve oneself or the
Government in the " shedding of blood." Clement of
Alexandria fled in his day; so did Polycarp; so did Cyprian.
Bishops ruled their churches from their hiding-places; it was
not their individual loss or gain that mattered, but the con-
venience and administration of the whole body. The earlier
maxim of St. Paul applied, a little altered : " Are you bound?
seek not to be loosed. Are you free? seek not to be bound."
None of these things *mattered*; all that mattered was belief,
prayer, love.

(ii) The question of the lapsed was the subject of much
discussion. If one, with or without torture, had denied
the Faith—what then? It was perhaps a more crucial question
than appears. By definition, the faithful *could* (in grace)
remain steadfast; and there could be no greater evil than to
deny, from fear or pain, the Way which was the basis of all
existence. If this was pardoned, anything could be pardoned,
for this was as near the sin against the Holy Ghost as was
normally shown to man. Yet pain and fear did distract and
break men, and—the Church swung towards mercy, and
towards a fuller realization of its own Nature, which is that
of redeemed sin. But the issue was complicated by a kind
of rash exchange on the part of those who had not failed.

As, for example, (iii) The confessors who escaped death
were regarded with a proper admiration by the rest of Christendom. They were supposed to have achieved by their
sufferings a sacerdotal power; priesthood was attributed to
them. A third-century document (the *Canons of Hippolytus*)
laid this down; confessors need not be ordained, for the
Holy Spirit had ordained them direct. They bestowed, on
occasion, formal absolution. Such a recognition was natural,
yet, if indeed the Church was to organize itself as an institution, it was highly dangerous. Not only did it tend to
introduce an irregular ministry, but it might easily have tended

to turn the regular ministry, so infiltrated by confessors, into
a superior spiritual grade. Besides making, as the Church
of Rome and Cyprian saw, confusion of another kind. A
man might have courage to be a confessor and even a martyr
without having the determination to be holy or even
virtuous. It was also held that the priesthood should be a
little educated, and confessors might or might not be educated.
At the cost of a good deal of dispute, the authorities carried
their point. Let confessors be ordained—as many as possible
and as quickly as possible. But unless ordained, let them
not exercise priestly functions. In the sacred order they might
have greater things, but those they had *not*. It was laid down
for ever that the administration of spiritual things does not
depend on the character of the administrator. A man may communicate to others, and himself starve; a man may preach to
others, and himself be a castaway.

In the Church of Carthage a remarkable situation arose.
It was encouraged by a local and clerical opposition to the
Bishop St. Cyprian, but it contained in itself the seeds of a
much greater doctrine—the common idea of substitution and
exchange: such as Felicitas had epigrammatized and Clement
had formulated. At Carthage the lapsed were many, and
there was a movement towards their complete and permanent
excommunication. Some of the repentant lapsed gave themselves up to the imperial magistrates. But the Carthaginian
Church also had its confessors, and recourse was had to
them on behalf of other sinners. The confessors were persuaded to " cover with their merits the demerits of the lapsed,
and to give *libelli pacis* for their readmission." The opposition
even put out an indulgence or absolution from " all the
confessors to all the lapsed," and desired Cyprian to promulgate it. Cyprian declined; it was against holy Order.
The universal Church, in Councils at Carthage and Rome, in
a Synod at Antioch, by the Bishop of Alexandria, followed
Cyprian's lead. It was indeed an impossible proposal, if the
Church as such was to retain any systematic control of its
members. Yet it was based on almost the profoundest secret

of all that the Church held, and centuries later the doctrine of the Treasury of Merits and the practice of indulgences was to popularize regularly the mysterious and irregular effort towards substitution made by the confessors of Carthage.

The last persecution of the third century took place in 257; under it Sixtus II was martyred in Rome while publicly teaching and Cyprian himself was beheaded at Carthage. But in 261 Gallienus revoked the edicts, and formally tolerated the Church : " let no one molest you." There was peace for forty years, with occasional partial exceptions. At the end of that time the " lord and god " Diocletian opened the greatest and last attack, the Tenth General Persecution.

Whatever the causes that led to it, the challenge was, in effect, final. It did not, at first, propose death; rather, it set the Faith again *hors de la loi.* It destroyed churches; it commanded the burning of all Christian Scriptures; it degraded all Christian officials. Presently it ordered that the clergy should be imprisoned. The attack was once more on the organization, and the intelligence of Diocletian refrained from re-inspiring enthusiasm by martyrdoms. Christendom was to expire from lack of nutrition; churches, documents, sacraments, were to be removed; public service was forbidden; the Faith was to be flung back on solitude, poverty, ignorance, inconvenience, suspicion, and contempt. Such had been the practice in some earlier attempts; it was renewed.

It is difficult not to read into the situation more than perhaps is justifiable; it is difficult also to refrain from seeing it as a parallel to events in our own day, especially when the labour and the genius of the Emperor are considered. He " restored order for a time in the Empire, defended the State from foreign enemies, set bounds to the raging current of passions and ambitions, and carried out a prudent and extensive programme of reform in public and private life." The historian who so describes him[3] goes on to attribute the failure of his efforts and of the Empire to a decline of

[3] *History of the Ancient World; Rome,* M. Rostovtzeff.

creative power. "Any creative power that remained turned
away from this world and its demands and studied how to
know God and be united with him." But that is hardly so;
it had been decided otherwise when the Gnostics were defeated and when time was found to be a necessary condition of
the Christian life. The new heresy of Manichæanism which
was intruding from the East might indeed exclude matter
and the world from its consideration. But the orthodox
Faith, based on the union of very matter with very deity,
could not do so. Its survival, its success, had partly been
due to its interlocked charity, its habits of exchange of all
wealth, its intense knowledge of the community. Its doctrines
were defined precisely by the common belief; its bishops,
for all their quarrels, were a federal college, half-appointed
by the specialists, half-elected by the crowd; its problems
were problems of the organization of time and the world. To
know God it was necessary to love the brethren—first, as it
were, from predilection and choice, but afterwards from
him and through him. "We love, because He loved us."
"If a man say that he love God and hateth his brother,
he is a liar and the truth is not in him." Felicitas had asserted
the divine order—"Another for me and I for him."
Clement had defined it among the faithful : "He demands of
us our lives for the sake of each other." What the martyr
and doctor declared another voice also proclaimed out of the
desert. During the reign of Diocletian St. Antony, the first
of the Christian hermits, whose life was to be written by
Athanasius, took up his dwelling between the Nile and the
Red Sea. Alone, ascetic, emaciated, he gave to the Church
the same formula : "Your life and your death are with your
neighbour."

Yet perhaps the greatest epigram of all is in a more
ambiguous phrase. Ignatius of Antioch in the early second
century, had tossed it out on his way to martyrdom : "My
Eros is crucified." Learned men have disputed on the exact
meaning of the word : can it refer, with its intensity of
allusion to physical passion, to Christ? or does it rather

refer to his own physical nature? We, who have too much separated our own physical nature from Christ's, cannot easily read an identity into the two meanings. But they unite, and others spring from them. " My love is crucified "; " My Love is crucified " : " My love for my Love is crucified "; " My Love in my love is crucified." The physical and the spiritual are no longer divided : he who is *Theos* is *Anthropos,* and all the images of *anthropos* are in him. The Eros that is crucified lives again and the Eros lives after a new style : this was the discovery of the operation of faith. The Eros of five hundred years of Greece and Rome was to live after a new style; unexpected as yet, the great Romantic vision approached. " *My* " Eros is crucified; incredible as yet, the great doctrines of interchange, of the City, approached. " Another is in me "; " your life and death are in your neighbour "; " they in Me and I in them."

From the extreme corner of the Empire, out beyond the Narrow Seas of Gaul, from Britain and the North, another figure was approaching. The Empire broke again into contending armies; the persecutions ceased, were renewed, hesitated, fell away, were renewed again. Six Augusti ruled the various provinces. Constantine, son of Constantius and Helena, afterwards a Christian, appeared in Gaul, and the Church there had peace. He crossed the Alps; one Augustus had been permitted by him to commit suicide at Marseilles, and now another fell in defeat at the Milvian Bridge. At Milan he made alliance with a third, Licinius. The Edict of Milan declared toleration of all religions; then the allied Augusti took measures against the fifth, Maximin, the persecutor of the East. Defeated at Adrianople, he fled back to Asia and in Cappadocia he too issued an edict of toleration. But the legions of the conquerors followed him; he fled to Tarsus, and there, while all over the Empire Christendom gave thanks for peace, the most furious of its enemies died in a raging delirium. Diocletian was also dead.

The two remaining Augusti recognized in full the existence of the Church; its worship was encouraged, its property was

restored. By the wording of the Edict of Milan it was not
the Church but the rest who were tolerated: "the open
and free exercise of their religion is granted to all others
as well as to the Christians." The operations of Constantine
encouraged—severely—the morals of the Christians, and
also unity in the Church. "Protection of all religions was fast
becoming patronage of one." Fornication and the Donatist
schism were alike heavily penalized; slaves gained a right
to eventual freedom, and criminals were no longer to be
branded on the face "because it is fashioned"—ordained the
Emperor, anticipating Dante—"after the similitude of the
heavenly beauty." His colleague leaned towards the old
gods. The breach between them was widened through ten
years; the war came, and in 323 Licinius died at Thessalonica.

Constantine was master of the Empire; he looked to be
more. "I am appointed," he said, "to be bishop of the
relations of the Church to the world at large." There were
disputes within the Church; they should be settled. He saw
himself already in the most difficult of all offices, the crowned
point of union between the supernatural and the natural.
He summoned the first General Council; at Nicaea more than
three hundred bishops met. They gathered in the large hall
of the imperial palace, and their imperial—but unbaptized—
patron appeared in his glory. "He appeared as a messenger
from God, covered with gold and precious stones—a magnificent figure, tall and slender, and full of grace and majesty,"
wrote the historian Eusebius. He blushed; he kept his eyes
on the ground; the bishops gestured towards him; he sat
down on the throne of gold; he spoke. He raised before
his audience a packet of letters of accusation written by
many against many; exhorting all to pardon, peace, and joy,
he solemnly burnt them. Then his Augustitude subdued
itself; theology began. Presently, after two months, the great
Assembly addressed the world.

The adorned figure of the Emperor, throned among the
thirty score of prelates, hearing and declaring with them the
witness of all the churches to the apostolic tradition, signifies

many things. There the acceptance of time was completely manifested; there a new basis—a metaphysical basis—was ordained for society. The Roman past was rejected; the effort of the Middle Ages was begun. Intellect was accepted; marriage was accepted; ordinary life was accepted. The early vision of St. Peter was found to have wider meanings than had been supposed: "what I have cleansed that call not thou common." The nature of the Church had not changed, and only fools suppose that it had. It remained reconciliation and sin redeemed; "my Eros is crucified"; "Another is in me." It was declared now by all the magnificence of this world, by the all-but-idol of the episcopate. It had become a Creed, and it remained a Gospel.

CHAPTER III

THE COMPENSATIONS OF SUCCESS

Christendom had set out to re-generate the world. The unregenerate Roman world was now handed over to it. No extreme difficulties were any longer to be put in its way, except under the noble but ill-fated effort of the Emperor Julian to restore the past. The old pagan rituals were not finally prohibited until the year 392, by Theodosius, and there was still a good deal of rhetorical and sincere opposition. But the no-man's land of religion, all the casual and fashionable sections of the Empire, became more or less formally Christian. All insincerity became Christian; neither Constantine nor the Church was to blame. Time had been a problem, and the Church had organized to deal with it; now space and numbers had become a similar problem. Christendom had been expanding within the Empire, and the acceleration had already become greater than the morality of Christendom could quite control. The acceleration and the corresponding loss of morality were highly increased.

Unfortunately they were so increased at the very moment when one of the profoundest divisions broke out—one can hardly say (by definition) within the Church, but within the apparent Church. The division had begun before Constantine; it was, in fact, the ostensible cause for the calling of Nicaea. Such divisions in the past had given opportunity for the activity of the worst emotions, even of sincere converts. The emotions of only half-sincere converts were even more damaging, and human destructiveness was loosed on a greater scale than ever before within the suddenly enlarged boundaries of Christendom. The grand Arian controversy had opened.

That this should have been possible at all, three centuries after Christ, shows how slow the Church had been towards exact dogmatic definition; it had been, and always has been, engaged on something else. Christ was the Redeemer, that was certain; and he was also, in some real sense, God; and, at least since the Montanists and Origen, there was a formal Trinity of Godhead. But in what sense was he God? in the same sense as the Father (allowing for the Persons)? or only in a similar sense to the Father? Was he co-eternal and co-equal? The alternative proposition was set forth by the persuasive, virtuous and ingenious deacon of Alexandria, Arius: "There was when He was not." If the Father was truly Father and Source, and the Son truly Son and Result, there must have been when he had not been. He was "of God," and the rest followed. It was as logical and simple as that.

The Synod of Alexandria conferred, and excommunicated Arius. He left the City. The bishop of Nicomedia and others received both him and his doctrine. The quarrel spread bitterly through the East. Both sides quoted Origen. The archdeacon of Alexandria, a small Egyptian named Athanasius, wrote against him on behalf of his bishop. The Emperor, hearing of the agitation, wrote letters to both sides pointing out that Christians ought to concentrate on living well: "he can't be wrong whose life is in the right." He deprecated disputes over formulæ. He can hardly be blamed. He had just defeated Licinius and restored peace and unity to the Roman world; he did not want his new Christian empire, its mobs and its magistrates, excited by abstract arguments. But the founder of a metaphysical empire has to put up with the drawbacks of the metaphysics. There had been civil wars in Rome, but none hitherto concerning the nature of the Godhead of the Emperor. But anything will do for a war. The world had been ready for its change, and Constantine had changed it. Three centuries of St. Paul's developed vocabulary had had their effect. Constantine's protest was natural; it was his misfortune that the point at issue should be one of the few more important and not one of the many less important. That is clear now; it was not everywhere equally clear then.

The Emperor summoned Nicaea; the Fathers got to work. The result is known. The question there asked was capable of translation into all categories, including the category of exchange. Was there, in the most Secret, in the only Adored —was there that which can be described only by such infelicitous mortal words as an equal relation, an equal goodwill, an equal love? was this in its very essence? was the Son co-eternal with the Father? If there had been no creation, would Love have practised love? and would Love have had an adequate object to love? Nicaea answered yes. It confirmed, beyond all creation, in the incomprehensible Alone, the cry of Felicitas: "Another is in Me." The Godhead itself was in Co-inherence. The doctrine of Arius had denied the possibility of equal exchange to God—outside creation. It is true that Arius, as well as Athanasius, held the other doctrine of free-will, and that in that sense every soul has it at choice to make exchange with God. But Nicaea went farther. Fourteen hundred years later, the doctrine was epigrammatized by an Anglican doctor when Dr. Hawarden, before the Queen of George II, asked Dr. Clarke: "Can God the Father annihilate God the Son?" That the question is, so to speak, meaningless is precisely the definition of orthodoxy. The Divine Son is not only "of God"; he is "God of God."

Nicaea then was a double climax. The spectacle of magnificence was accompanied by an intellectual ostentation of dogma. "The great and sacred Synod" exhibited itself in the two worlds. Christ was throned in heaven and in Constantinople. Yet at times, as the jewels seem only jewels, so the words seem only words. "Father," "Son," "Holy Spirit," "Person," "essence and nature," "like and unlike" —what has such a pattern of definition to do with a Being that must exist always in its own incomprehensibility? It is not surprising that the human mind should revolt against the jewels and words. It is, of course, a revolt of immature sensibility, an ignorant, a young-romantic revolt, but it is natural. "The great and sacred Synod" looms sublimely

anti-pathetic. From such revolts there have sprung the equally
immature and romantic devotions to the simple Jesus, the
spiritual genius, the broad-minded international Jewish work-
ing-man, the falling-sparrow and grass-of-the-field Jesus. They
will not serve. The Christian idea from the beginning had
believed that his Nature reconciled earth and heaven, and
all things met in him, God and Man. A Confucian Wordsworth
does not help there. Jewels and words are but images, but
then so are grass and sparrows. And jewels and words are no
less and no more necessary than cotton and silence.

Yet Christendom had felt the revolt even before Nicaea—
only not as a revolt, but as a compensating movement.
Antony had gone out into the desert and many had followed
him. He had organized them, and away in south Egypt
another hermit, Pachomius, had done the same thing for
other bands. The great and sacred labour in the imperial
palace was balanced by the sacred and ascetic labour of the
solitaries. Sleep and food and drink and clothing were
reduced to the barest needs—and to less. A rivalry in repudiation ran about the desert, and the rumours of the gaunt and
holy figures of its practitioners percolated through the bazaars
of the great cities. "The sign of the solitary ascetics" wrote
Athanasius (the Athanasius of Nicaea, of Alexandria, of
humanism, of the Court and the Church) in his *Life of Antony,*
"rules from one end of the earth to the other." It dominated
the impressionable everywhere; it was said (improbably)
that in one city were "more than two thousand virgins leading lives of ascetic excellence." Many more admired it than
practised it, but many practised it. The notion of the way of
complete rejection, of the reduction of both soul and body
to as near a state of nothingness under God as might be
won—gained strangely on life. The huts, the caves, the
pillars of the ascetics did indeed hold those who concen-
trated on nothing but their relation with God, to whom the
whole outer world and (but for one thought) the whole inner
world had become temptation. New temptations at once
sprung up—of rivalry, of pride, of *accidia.* But even the

wild tales we have show how they too were recognized and denounced. "God hath not forgiven thee thy sins," said the hermit Bessarion to the harlot Thais, "because of thy repentance but because of thy thought to deliver thyself to Christ." And so a certain Elijah said: "Whatsoever hath its being for God's sake endureth and abideth for ever with those who are true."

Exchange therefore to them was always on the Way and as between hurrying travellers. It was an exchange of humility and tenderness and (often) of remarkable intelligence. A danger, more obvious perhaps to us than to them, was in their awareness of virtue; they have sometimes that sense of strain which the author of *The Cloud of Unknowing* in a later century denounced. It is why they saw the devil so often. Their comments on humility examine that virtue too feverishly to be quite convincing. But the greatest of them were peculiarly lucid. Macarius said to Arsenius: "I know a brother who had a few garden herbs in his cell, and to prevent himself having any sense of gratification, he pulled them up by the roots." Arsenius answered: "Good, but a man must do as he is able, and if he is not strong enough to endure, perhaps he should plant others." They knew also the remote principle. A certain brother said: "It is right for a man to take up the burden for them who are near to him, whatever it may be, and, so to speak, to put his own soul in the place of that of his neighbour, and to become, if it were possible, a double man, and he must suffer, and weep, and mourn with him, and finally the matter must be accounted by him as if he himself had put on the actual body of his neighbour, and as if he had acquired his countenance and soul, and he must suffer for him as he would for himself. For thus it is written *We are all one body*, and this passage also informs us concerning the holy and mysterious kiss."

The old Gnostic view that matter was evil had no doubt affected them, and the newer Gnosticism that had begun, in the form of Manichæanism, to sweep inward from the East. It had been forbidden by Diocletian as un-European, as a Persian import, before it was rejected by Christendom as un-Christian, as a diabolic luxury. But of all the heresies it is one of the few most generally and most subtly nourished by our common natures. There is in it always a renewed emotional energy. It is due to Manichæanism that there has grown up in Christendom—in spite of the myth of the Fall in Genesis—the vague suggestion that the body has somehow fallen farther than the soul. It was certainly nourished within the Church by the desert ascetics—especially in their ingenuous repudiation of sex. This is probably the one thing generally known about them—except for the pillar of St. Simeon Stylites—and the contempt and hatred they too rashly expressed for it has been heartily reciprocated against them by a later world. It was no more than a part of their general passion for singleness of soul, even when that singleness tended to become a singularity. Sex—the poor ignorant creatures thought—was one of the greatest, most subtle, and most lasting of all distractions; nor had the Church—at least since the suppression of the *sub-introductæ*—shown any striking sign of intending to exhibit it as sometimes the greatest, most splendid, and most authoritative of all inducements. Yet even in the Thebaid the rejection was, at best, regarded as no more than a method of the Way. " A monk met the handmaids of God upon a mountain road, and at the sight of them he turned out of the way. And the Abbess said to him : ' Hadst thou been a perfect monk thou wouldst not have looked so close as to perceive we were women.' "[1] The answer would have been perfect if she had said " Thou wouldst not have perceived we were women." Perhaps she did.

There is, no doubt, a lordlier state than that, to observe with adoration all shapes, including women; but the rebuke was—or at least may have been—charming, and exhibits, in the desert as in the city, the desire which is the Glory of

[1] *The Desert Fathers,* Helen Waddell. (The other quotations are from *The Paradise of the Fathers,* E. A. Wallis Budge.)

Christendom. "Look," said the first founder when he lay dying, "Antony ends *his* journey; he goes now wherever Divine Grace shall bring him."

Counterchecking the asceticism it admired, the formal doctrine of Christendom concerning matter remained constant. Two ancient canons, said to date from the second or third century, illuminate the official view. They run as follows: "If any bishop or priest or deacon, or any cleric whatsoever, shall refrain from marriage and from meat and from wine, not for the sake of discipline but with contempt, and, forgetful that all things are very good and that God made man male and female, blasphemously inveighs against the creation (*blasphemans accusaverit creationem*), let him be either corrected or deposed and turned out of the Church (*atque ex Ecclesia ejiciatur*). And so with a layman."

"If any bishop or priest or deacon does no feed on meat and wine on feast days, let him be deposed, lest he have his own conscience hardened, and be a cause of scandal to many."[2]

"Blasphemously inveighing against the creation"—if the whole of Christendom had taken to the desert and lived among the lions, it remained true that the authority of the pillared pontiffs would have been compelled to assert that marriage and meat and wine were "*valde bona.*" Rejection was to be rejection but not denial, as reception was to be reception but not subservience. Both methods, the Affirmative Way and the Negative Way, were to co-exist; one might almost say, to co-inhere, since each was to be the key of the other: in intellect as in emotion, in morals as in doctrine. "Your life and your death are with your neighbour." No Affirmation could be so complete as not to need definition, discipline, and refusal; no Rejection so absolute as not to leave necessary (literally and metaphorically) beans and a wild beast's skin and a little water. Those who most rejected material things might cling the more closely to verbal formulæ; those who looked most askance at the formulæ

[2] *History of the Church Councils*, Hefele; the Greek original is there translated into Latin.

might apprehend most easily the divine imagery of matter. The Communion of the Eucharist, at once an image and a Presence, was common and necessary to both. The one Way was to affirm all things orderly until the universe throbbed with vitality; the other to reject all things until there was nothing anywhere but He. The Way of Affirmation was to develop great art and romantic love and marriage and philosophy and social justice; the Way of Rejection was to break out continually in the profound mystical documents of the soul, the records of the great psychological masters of Christendom. All was involved in Christendom, and between them, as it were, hummed the web of the ecclesiastical hierarchy, labouring, ordering, expressing, confirming, and often misunderstanding, but necessary to any organization in time and particularly necessary at that time in the recently expanded space.

There are two documents, of a date later by a century or two, which present the division between the Ways in the world of definitions, and as regards the Nature of God. One is the great humanist Ode " commonly called the Creed of St. Athanasius "; the other is the *Mystical Theology* of Dionysius the Areopagite. Certainly the Creed talks about Incomprehensibility and Dionysius plans out the heavens. Neither document sustains the view of Eunomius bishop of Cyzicus, who " changed theology into technology " and is reported to have declared : " I know God as well as He knows Himself."[3] But the objective " humanist " may serve for a division; the climax of the one is what is known, allowing the unknown; of the other what must be unknown, allowing the known. The union of both is in the phrase of Ignatius, quoted by Dionysius and dogmatically declared in the Creed : " My Love is crucified."

The Creed is the definition of salvation, and it lays down a primal necessary condition—that one shall believe in the existence of salvation and in its own proper nature. It does not go back to that other demand for a decision of belief in

[3] *History of the Christian Church,* Kidd.

one's own existence which is almost always a desirable preliminary. One feels, one thinks, that one exists, but one hardly ever makes a serious act of belief in one's existence, whereas it might be held that a proper Christendom would be composed of people who believe that, through God, they exist but do not noticeably think or feel it. The Athanasian Creed, however, being a more advanced document, begins with the Creator. It sums up in those crossing and clamorous clauses all the business of Relationship in Deity; Deity, so, is one God—the word triumphs over the reduced plural: "there are not three gods, but one God." Thence it proceeds to the Incarnation: "it is necessary that he believe rightly." It is in this connection that it produces a phrase which is the very maxim of the Affirmative Way: "Not by conversion of the Godhead into flesh but by taking of the manhood into God." And not only of the particular religious Way, but of all progress of all affirmations: it is the actual manhood which is to be carried on, and not the height which is to be brought down. All images are, in their degree, to be carried on; mind is never to put off matter; all experience is to be gathered in. Images can be as disciplinary as their lack; their rejection itself can be a temptation. By the Substitution and the Sacrifice, the "good works" are all to be prolonged and gathered, and those who share in it are to find it eternal life. This is the principle which is to be kept "whole and un-defiled"; and who can? no; therefore it will keep itself, it will correct and illuminate itself; without that grand union —"perfect God and perfect Man; of a reasonable soul and human flesh subsisting"—man is bound to slip from vanity to vanity, from illusion to illusion, everlastingly perishing, ever-lastingly lost. "But the Catholic Faith is this . . ."

The other document is very different.

In the year 533 at Constantinople, the Patriarch of Antioch, Severus, a Monophysite, spoke of the writings of Dionysius the Areopagite. The books which thus heretically invoked had at that time, as so many other writings had, an authority almost apostolic incorrectly attributed to them; to say "falsely" would imply a moral intention of which no one then thought. Dionysius, it was supposed, was an Athenian, a direct disciple of St. Paul, and (by his ordination) first bishop of Athens. He had produced a book on the Heavenly Hierarchy, and one on the Ecclesiastical, one on the Divine Names and one on Mystical Theology. It is now thought likely that he was a Syrian monk of the late fifth century, and a disciple of one Hierotheus, more or less identified with another Syrian, Stephen bar Sudaili. From the year 533 these writings have always hovered over Christendom almost like the unfooted Bird of Paradise— admired, worshipped, and yet by some distrusted. He was invoked as orthodox by Pope Victor I at the Lateran Council in 649; in 757 his books were sent by Pope Paul to the Church in Gaul; and the Emperor of the East Michael Balbus sent them also to Louis the Pious. They were translated, for Charles the Bald of France and for the West, by John Scotus Erigena. St. John Damascene had learnt from and annotated them; in the full power of Scholasticism Aquinas quoted from them as from any other doctor of perpetual authority in the Church, and the anonymous author of the *Cloud of Unknowing*, in his sublime rejection of images, and as he wrote of the final failing even of spiritual wit in the presence of the Alone, remembered one paragraph of Dionysius to confirm his own last cry.

They are, in fact, the climax of one great mode of speculation and of experience; they are hardly, yet they are, within the orthodoxy of Christendom. They provide the great negative definitions infinitely satisfying to a certain type of mind when it contemplates intellectually the Divine Principle. The conclusion of the *Mystical Theology* soars into the great darkness, lit faintly by the very phrases it rejects.

Once more, ascending yet higher, we maintain that It is not soul, or mind, or endowed with the faculty of imagination, conjecture, reason, or understanding; nor is It any act of reason or understanding; nor can It be described by the reason or perceived by the understanding, since It is not number, or order, or greatness, or littleness, or equality, or inequality, and since It is not immovable nor in motion, or at rest, and has no power, and is not power or light, and does not live, and is not life; nor is It personal essence, or eternity, or time; nor can It be grasped by the understanding, since It is not knowledge or truth; nor is It kingship or wisdom; nor is It one, nor is It unity, nor is It Godhead or Goodness; nor is It a Spirit, as we understand the term, since It is not Sonship or Fatherhood; nor is It any other thing such as we or any other being can have knowledge of; nor does It belong to the category of non-existence or to that of existence; nor do existent beings know It as it actually is, nor does It know them as they actually are; nor can the reason attain to It to name It or to know It; nor is It darkness, nor is It light, or error, or truth; nor can any affirmation or negation apply to it; for while applying affirmations or negations to those orders of being that come next to It, we apply not unto It either affirmation or negation, inasmuch as It transcends all affirmation by being the perfect and unique Cause of all things, and transcends all negation by the pre-eminence of Its simple and absolute nature—free from every limitation and beyond them all.

It has been said that this is not the kind of being to whom man can pray; no, but without this revelation there is no sort of thing to whom men can *pray,* and the orisons of Christendom will be too much circumscribed. And Dionysius himself knew the other Way, and his book on the *Divine Names* is more akin to it—as when he refers to St. Paul, in its discussion of " My Eros is crucified." " And hence the great Paul, constrained by the Divine Yearning . . . says, with inspired utterance: 'I live, and yet not I but Christ liveth in me '; true Sweetheart that he was and (as he says himself) being beside himself unto God and not possessing his own life but possessing the life of Him for whom he yearned." For that which is beyond all categories and has only within itself its necessity of being, " is touched by the sweet spell of Goodness, Love, and Yearning, and so is drawn from his transcendent throne above all things, to dwell within the heart of all things, through a super-essential and ecstatic power whereby he yet stays within himself."[4]

Yet perhaps neither the Egyptian hermits and monks nor the Syrians on their interior " top of speculation " are the true compensation and balance of Nicaea, quite apart from the disturbances, riots, exiles and excommunications which immediately followed Nicaea. The Arians split into Arians and semi-Arians; the declarations of the " great and sacred Synod " were hotly disputed, and if the Holy Spirit had there controlled the voice, he did not attempt to silence the voices, of Christendom. Bishops were banished and recalled; the Emperor swayed dangerously near the more understandable Arian point of view; Athanasius became Bishop of Alexandria and fled and returned and was driven out. He took refuge with the desert monks who were fanatically orthodox. Arius came back to Alexandria, fell from his mule, and died, but his death did not put an end to his doctrine. Accidents to such distinguished leaders were, to their opponents, nearly always miracles of judgment, and during this period there was encouraged in Christendom the view which attempted to discern in exterior events an index to interior and spiritual truth; the false devotion which in a later day invented terrifying death-beds for atheists and agonizing diseases for Sabbath-breakers. This in itself is dangerous enough; it is made worse by that fatal tendency in men to hasten God's work and to supply, on his behalf, the deaths and the agonies which they think his inscrutable patience has rashly postponed. So fomented into fire and bloodshed the Arian controversy pursued its way through Constantine's otherwise peaceful empire.

This, however, was the result of Nicaea. About the middle of the century, about the time of the death of Antony and the third exile of Athanasius, the real compensation

[4] *Dionysius the Areopagite,* C. E. Rolt.

to Nicaea was born at Thagaste in Numidia; its name was
Augustine. He came to redress (or, as some have thought,
to upset for ever) the balance of the Church. Speculation
had, in the East, ascended from the foot of the imperial
throne to the height of the heavenly, and the idea of exchange
had been followed into the extremest corners of heaven. With
Augustine theology returned to man and to sin. The Church
had always known about sin; some of her doctors (as
Tertullian) knew a great deal about it. But on the whole,
especially since the Alexandrian doctors, she had stressed
the Redemption. So, no doubt, did Augustine; read the
Confessions. Yet those very *Confessions* seem to contain
everything except one thing, the *anima naturaliter Christiana*.
They divide, in an agony, the natural body from the spiritual
body, and their readers and followers have divided even
more fervently. When St. Monica drove Augustine's eighteen-
years paramour, the mother of his son, back from Milan
to Africa, something went with her which perhaps Christendom and Augustine needed almost as much as they needed
St. Monica, though not as much as Christendom needed
Augustine. Christendom did not then get her. It got the
style of Augustine instead, and that style never seemed quite
to apprehend that a man could grow, sweetly and naturally
—and no less naturally and sweetly in spite of all the stages
of repentance necessarily involved—from man into new man.
He certainly is the less likely to do so who dwells much on
the possibility. But the movement exists and the great
Augustinian energy of conversion, contrition, and aspiration
lies a little on one side of it. Formally Augustine did not
err; but informally? He also, for all his culture, followed
the Way of Rejection of Images, and he inspired later
centuries to return to that Way. He has always been a
danger to the devout, for without his genius they lose
his scope. Move some of his sayings but a little from the
centre of his passion and they point to damnation. The
anthropos that is Christ becomes half-hidden by the *anthropos*
that was Adam. In Augustine this did not happen, for his

eyes were fixed on Christ. But he almost succeeded, in fact though not in intention, in dangerously directing the eyes of Christendom to Adam.

" Augustine, from his small seaport on the North African coast, swayed the whole Western Church as its intellectual dictator."[5] He had been converted like St. Paul; he had seized Christ through Paul. He rose into Christendom from what seemed to him catastrophes. And the great primal catastrophe was the situation into which every man was born; the New Birth was the freedom from that catastrophe. Two famous sayings epigrammatize the change. The first is the reluctant sigh: " Make me chaste, my Lord, but not yet!" The second is the reconciled joy: " Command chastity; give what thou commandest, and command what thou wilt!" Both come from the *Confessions,* which (Augustine said scornfully) men read from curiosity, or (he might have added) from a human sense of the human; it is not what that great Refuser of Images wished. Few things seemed to him more imbecile than that his autobiography should be admired for everything except the whole conclusion, climax, and cause of his autobiography. But a phrase in it—the second of the two quoted—was permitted by our Lord the Spirit to become the occasion of more controversy and of high decision in Christendom.

There was a meeting in Rome—perhaps a clerical conference or something of the kind. A certain Pelagius, an Irish Christian, was present at it. He was not a priest but he was in Rome on an effort to revive and excite religion; he was conducting a mission to the Romans. His particular method was to encourage men to be *men.* He was orthodox enough, and full of a real love for, and desire for the good of, his fellow-creatures, but he thought his fellow-creatures were perfectly capable of fulfilling the Will of God and of being chaste (or whatever) if they wished. Men need not sin unless they chose, and if they did not choose they need not sin. This too was orthodox enough. He had had

[5] *The Idea of the Fall,* N. P. Williams.

D.D.   C

some success, and his influence was spreading. At this meeting there was " a certain brother, a fellow-bishop of mine," says Augustine. The bishop during the meeting quoted from the *Confessions,* already in wide circulation, the phrase: " *da quod iubes,*" " give what thou commandest." This, Augustine adds, *Pelagius ferre non potuit*— Pelagius simply could not stand that sort of thing. Man was not in that kind of situation at all; no doubt he was tempted, but he could resist temptation. " Pull yourself together, my dear fellow," he said in effect, and he actually did say that to talk of virtue being hard or difficult, or to say it could not be done, or to moan about the weakness of the flesh was to contradict God flatly, and to pretend either that he did not know what he had made or did not understand what he was commanding: " as if . . . he had forced upon man commands man could not endure."

But this, which to Pelagius seemed so scandalous, seemed to Augustine merely truth. Chaste was what the law had bidden him to be and what he had not been able to be. The law was precisely impossible. Man precisely was not *in* a situation—not even in a difficult situation. He was, himself, the situation; he was, himself, the contradiction; he was, himself, death-in-life and life-in-death. He was incompetent. Augustine had felt that acutely; since his conversion he had been teaching it—that man was the situation and only the grace of God could alter the situation. Both Pelagius and he felt strongly the desirability of man overcoming sin, but the problem was what was sin and how best did you overcome it. The expanding circles of doctrine spread outward from Rome and Hippo. Never before had Christendom felt the two views so fully and so honestly developed. It had previously accepted a general notion that men were in a " fallen " state, but it had not pressed any definition of it. What definitions it had produced had tended to relate to the Person who redeemed men from the state. That, after all, was what its greatest minds and noblest souls had been concerned with. The clash of Pelagius and Augustine altered all that.

That man, in the person of Adam, had fallen was common ground. Pelagius said, in effect, that (i) Adam had been created in a state of natural good, (ii) that he had somehow sinned, and set a bad example of sinning, so that a sort of social habit of sin had developed, into which men were introduced as they grew up before they were reasonable, (iii) but that any man at any moment could get out of this distressing social habit by simply being firm with himself —" have courage, my boy, to say no," (iv) and that therefore no particular grace of God was needed to initiate the change, though that grace was a convenient and necessary help : which was always to be found by the right-willing man.

Against this the Augustinian view—with the great help of Augustine himself—asserted (i) that man was created in a state of supernatural good, of specific awareness of God, (ii) that Adam had got himself out of that state by sin, and his sin was " pride "—that is, " the act of deserting the soul's true ' principle ' and constituting oneself one's own principle."[6] He had, as it were, claimed to have, and behaved as if he had, a necessity of being in himself. He had, somehow and somewhere, behaved as if he were God. (iii) His descendants therefore were not at all in a mere social habit of sinning; they did not merely sometimes sin; they were sinners, which was not at all the same thing. Nay, more, they had, all of them, been involved in that first original iniquity, and in its guilt. " *Omnes enim fuimus in illo uno quando omnes fuimus ille unus* "—we were all in that one man when we all were that one man. Thus, being all guilty, we all deserved, and were on our way to, hell by the mere business of getting ourselves born, though not, of course, *for* getting ourselves born. This was precisely the agony : to be born was good, but that good meant the utmost evil, life-into-death and death-into-life. Some who managed to die again before the age of reason might suffer less thereafter. But for the rest men were *corrupt*; they existed in the night of dreadful

[6] *St. Augustine and French Classical Thought*, Nigel Abercrombie.

ignorance and the storm of perverse love; they were for ever and ever sharers in that primal catastrophe which was the result of Adam imagining that he had a principle and necessity of existence within himself. (iv) It was therefore blasphemous and heretical nonsense to talk of man as being mildly and socially habituated to sin: he was in sin, and he could not get out by his own choice. He could not move but by grace, by that principle which was not in him. To Augustine Pelagius was practically teaching men to follow, to plunge deeper into, that old original catastrophe; he was almost declaring that man was his own principle, that he did his own good deeds. But all Christendom, and especially Augustine, knew that only Christ could act Christ.

But if only Christ acts Christ, who acts Anti-Christ? If all our good doing is God's doing, whose is our evil doing? Ours? Yes. God, as it were, determines and predestinates himself to do good in certain lives; this is his grace. And what of the lives in which he does not determine and predestinate himself to do good? Well—he does not. Those lives then are lost? Well—yes. God saves whom he chooses and the rest damn themselves. " His equity is so secret that it is beyond the reach of all human understanding." It is of the highest importance to realize that, in that sentence, Augustine from the bottom of his heart meant " equity " and meant " beyond human understanding."

" The first modern," as Augustine has been called, had uttered the word " grace " with a new accent. Adam had suddenly returned. " The grace of our Lord Jesus Christ " was to be analysed and discussed as the Nature of our Lord Jesus Christ had been. The secrets of man's corruption were to become as much a matter for the brooding intellect of Christendom as the secrets of his Redemption had been. The inclusion of the Saviour in the Godhead was followed by the exclusion of Adam to the opening, at least, of the pit, and of all his children whom the unpredictable Equity did not choose out of so many myriads to redeem. Yet it may be noticed that Augustine, perhaps to the danger of his own thought, and certainly to the danger of the thought of his successors, was aiming at the same principle of inevitable relationship which in so many other things governed the orthodoxy of the Church. *" Fuimus ille unus "* he said; " we were in the one when we were the one." Whatever ages of time lay between us and Adam, yet we were in him and we were he; more, we sinned in him and his guilt is in us. And if indeed all mankind is held together by its web of existence, then ages cannot separate one from another. Exchange, substitution, co-inherence are a natural fact as well as a supernatural truth. "Another is in me," said Felicitas; " we were in another," said Augustine. The co-inherence reaches back to the beginning as it stretches on to the end, and the *anthropos* is present everywhere. " As in Adam all die, even so in Christ shall all be made alive "; co-inherence did not begin with Christianity; all that happened then was that co-inherence itself was redeemed and revealed by that very redemption as a supernatural principle as well as a natural. We were made sin in Adam but Christ was made sin for us and we in him were taken out of sin. To refuse the ancient heritage of guilt is to cut ourselves off from man-kind as certainly as to refuse the new principle. It is necessary to submit to the one as freely as to the other.

The new principle had been introduced into the web, and only that principle could separate one soul from another or any soul from the multitude. The principle was not only in the spirit but in the flesh of man. Pelagius declared that man had moral freedom, as Nestorius later declared that there were in Christ two beings united by a moral union and not one divine Person. " The Nestorian God is the fitting Saviour of the Pelagian man."[7] It was this that caused Nestorius to deny that the Blessed Virgin was *theotokos,* the mother of God. But he denied also, inevitably, that she was *anthropotokos,* the mother of Man. The opposite school maintained that she was both, for both the Fall and the Redemption were in

[7] *Our Lord's Human Example,* W. Gore; quoted by N. P. Williams, *The Idea of the Fall.*

soul and body. The mystery was in flesh and blood. It was this profundity of exchange and substitution, natural and supernatural, that the zeal of Augustine profoundly declared through Christendom. Christendom never quite committed itself to Augustine; it has spent centuries escaping from the phrases of Augustine. But without Augustine it might have ceased to be Christendom.

He did more. He did much more. " Seen against Christian philosophy as a whole even thinkers like Clement and Origen are only forerunners of Augustine; for they philosophize about God and human nature, but not about the divine sphere, the sphere of communion with God, which did not exist as a problem for the philosophical consciousness before the *Civitas Dei.*"[8] It was not only the book called by that name which was the expression of that thing, nor only that Augustine was imagining a heavenly state. A hundred apocrypha of the apocalypse had imagined *that*; the Church had never paused in affirming *that*. There were in Augustine two points of farther greatness. He had carried the Redemption back, as it were, in man's nature almost—quite—to the point at which man's error began. The very sin which a man had committed in Adam before his own birth was the starting-point of the predestinating grace which, before his own birth, awaited the moment of his birth to begin its immediate operation. The City of God leaps upon its citizens, presiding like the god Vaticanus over the first wail of the child, separating it for ever from the transient earthly cities, making it a pilgrim and a sojourner. The Equity of Redemption is immediately at work; it predestinates whom it chooses, and it does not predestinate whom it does not choose. But its choice is (beyond human thought) inextricably mingled with each man's own choice. It wills what he wills, because it has freedom to do so. Predestination is the other side of its own freedom. Words fall away from the inscrutable union, which can be the inscrutable separation.

[8] " Platonism in Augustine's Philosophy of History," Ernst Hoffman (*Philosophy and History*, edited by R. Klibansky and H. J. Paton).

And this heavenly state was a sphere of operation. The equity of predestination was to a state of love. Augustine gave his genius not to a description but to a suggestion of that *state* of love. The sensibility of the *Confessions* vibrates with this; the universals of the City of God make an effort to diagrammatize its relation with history—that is, with time as known by man. He hypothesized history into the workings of the Divine Providence, and the hypothesis has been, intellectually, made too often merely dull. But the real significance was in the vast accident, the vast sense of opportunity. It is Augustine's sense of opportunity which springs active everywhere, and everywhere that dash of vision opens on all that opportunity holds. Christ had been the opportunity; St. Paul had formed a vocabulary for that opportunity; Augustine turned the vocabulary into a language, a diction, a style. The Athanasian speech was the more highly specialized, Augustine's the more universal. He renewed the good news—man was utterly corrupt, and his scope was love. He renewed the City; he made humility possible for all. "Perfection consists not in what we give to God but in what we receive from him."[9]

The exterior crisis of the world in his age exposes to us that expansion of the Apostolic word at the moment when the world was ruining. On 24 August, in the year of the City 1164 and in the year of the Fructiferous Incarnation 410, the Goths under Alaric entered and sacked Rome. "My voice sticks in my throat," said Jerome, "and sobs choke me as I dictate. The City which took the whole world captive is itself taken." He uttered the sensations of all, both Christians and heathen. There has been no such shock to Europe since. Refugees fled to Sicily, to Syria, to Africa (Pelagius among the last; Augustine saw him in Carthage). Twenty years later, "in the seventy-sixth year of his age and the thirty-fifth of his episcopate, Augustine died, 28 August, 430, his eyes

[9] *The Life of the Church*, edited by M. D'Arcy, s.j. Bk. ii; *Christianity and the Soul of Antiquity*, by P. Rousselot, s.j. and J. Herby, s.j.

fixed on the penitential psalms and the sound of a besieging host of Vandals in his ears. . . . They offered the Holy Sacrifice at his burial."[10]   It was the summary and consummation of his life and doctrine; he had saved Christendom at the moment when Honorius, Emperor of the West, lost Rome.

[10] *History of the Church*, Kidd.

CHAPTER IV

THE WAR OF THE FRONTIERS

Not many years after the fall of Rome, the last Emperor of the West died at Ravenna. The few Senators who were with him escaped from Italy, and at Byzantium laid the fealty of the West at the foot of the Throne. The Empire was again one, as it had been in the days of the Divine Augustus.

But the differences from that early state were many. The alteration of the centre had changed the frontiers. Italy itself was now a frontier to the Government at Byzantium and Gaul was not much more than a distant No-man's-land of battle. Persia and the Near East were now the peril, though so far it was a secular prestige only which threatened the secular and sacred Emperor. Another two centuries were to pass before the voice of the Prophet would begin to sound nearer and nearer to New Rome. The ancient idea of Rome had been translated into a new language of which the chief and most resounding word was the living form of the Emperor, " the Basileus High-Priest," " the chief Bishop outside the Church," the single figure in which were exhibited the two complementary offices of men, sacred and secular, as the two Natures had been united in Christ. The Throne and the City were to last for a thousand years, and when they fell at last they were to fall not to any rebellious principate or patriarchate of the West, but to the Eastern despot who expressed in his own person the separation of the Two Natures as the Emperor expressed their union.

While, however, in the East there appeared the succession of almost pontiff-emperors in the new Rome, the deserted and desecrated city of old Rome was left practically to its poor and its Bishop. The flight of the notables before Alaric had left it " empty " for the return of the Pope

Innocent I from his negotiations at Ravenna, and in the new fashion of the Empire his authority stood high, and the higher that in the West there was but one see of such an eminence. The thrones of Antioch, Alexandria, Jerusalem, rivalled each other in the East, but from the Ægean to the North Sea there was but the one Apostolic Chair. Its secular prestige had sunk a little since the Removal, just as the secular prestige of Byzantium had gone up. The see of Byzantium had been no more than episcopal until the establishment there of the centre of the Empire, but the dignity of the Emperor demanded something greater to salute or to overawe, and at the Council of Constantinople (381) the See was ordered to take precedence next after Rome. The actual title of Patriarch was not given till the Council of Chalcedon.

But apart from such semi-diplomatic moves the See of Rome had its own peculiar tradition of judgment. Its political and apostolic prestige had already, in the early centuries of the Church, made it a particular test of orthodoxy. The Faith was made and maintained by the common consent of the Church, and of that assent the bishops were the guardians. *Quis custodiet custodes?* In all disputes the answer, on one side or the other, tended more and more to be *Rome,* and the support of whichever side by the Roman Bishop gave to that side a great, though not always a decisive, advantage. Saints and theologians often disagreed with her and sometimes denounced her, but her bishops received from the length and breadth of the Empire appeals to which at last they were asserting a divine right.

In the West all roads, at least of controversy, led to Rome; and if in the East they sometimes tended towards other cities and even to General Councils—Constantinople, Chalcedon, Ephesus—it remained that the roads which in turn came to such points from Rome came from the whole of the West. The delicate subtleties of Greek theological thought were not always appreciated in Italy, but decision was more easy to the Latin mind than argument, and the firmness of the Roman sentence had always eastern Adullamites to support it. (Such a development leaves, of course, the supernatural hypothesis of the Apostolic See untouched.)

The tiara of the pontiff-Emperor and the tiara of the Roman Bishop arose above the new world. But there were other and more spectacular changes, some of them particular, as in the ritual about the Emperor, some general, as in the alteration of crosses. When St. Paul preached in Athens, the world was thronged with crosses, rooted outside cities, bearing all of them the bodies of slowly dying men. When Augustine preached in Carthage, the world was also thronged with crosses, but now in the very centre of cities, lifted in processions and above altars, decorated and jewelled, and bearing all of them the image of the Identity of dying Man. There can hardly ever have been—it is a platitude— a more astonishing reversion in the history of the world. It is not surprising that Christianity should sometimes be regarded as the darkest of superstitions, when it is considered that a thing of the lowest and most indecent horror should have been lifted, lit, and monstrously adored, and that not merely sensationally but by the vivid and philosophic assent of the great intellects of the Roman world. The worship in jungles and marshes, the intoxication of Oriental mysteries, had not hidden in incense and litany a more shocking idol. The bloody and mutilated Form went up everywhere; Justinian built the Church of Holy Wisdom to it in Byzantium, and the Pope sang Mass before it on the hills where Rome had been founded. The jewelled crosses hid one thing only—they hid the indecency. But original crucifixion was precisely indecent. The images we still retain conceal—perhaps necessarily— the same thing; they preserve pain but they lack obscenity. But the dying agony of the God-Man exhibited both; depth below depth of meaning lies in that phrase—" My Eros is crucified."

Yet if the image was ghastly and horrible, the sacrificers were not so. There were still many altars, as there had been before, but the old republican worship of household gods had disappeared, and the pouring of honourable libations. The

East had overcome Rome, as the civic fathers had feared it might when they forbade Cybele to enter the City. But the East itself had changed in doing so. There was offered everywhere " the clean sacrifice." Men were no longer to die, for Man had died; orgies were no longer mystically to celebrate divine nuptials, for that must be a secret process of arduous will; ecstasy was no longer specially to be desired, for the ordinary daylight was as much He as the extraordinary night. Even the dark night of the soul was, as it were, nothing out of the common. Dullness, as well as drama, was to be borne on the wings of the spirit, and the Church leaned strongly to the idea that dullness was more reliable than drama. It had been, in fact, one of the objections to the Faith that it originally offered itself particularly to slaves and small shopkeepers. Its modern antagonists denounce it still as a bourgeois superstition; and certainly St. Paul and St. Augustine themselves demanded precisely that their converts should become the bourgeoisie of a City. The difficulty has generally been to prevent the bourgeois mind from supposing that it satisfactorily understood all the heavenly experiences which the bourgeois soul endured.

There had been, so far, little dispute on the nature of the Eucharistic Food. The Rite, with some variation of ceremony, was the same everywhere—from Delphi to Mona, from Carthage to Antioch. The elements of the Bread and the Wine were presented, the invocation of the God corresponded with His will and obeyed His command; the elements underwent His pre-occupation, and the original actuality of the Death of Messias in some way existed among the faithful. By virtue of that Death they communicated upon Him living. The Death was not repeated, for that could not be. As the Church accommodated herself to time in her dealing with the world so she also receded out of time in her union with her Victim and her Way. He had commanded her to command him, and she did; there, in the *here and now* of each particular Rite, holy exchange was perfected. She communicated and she adored.

But if, all over the Empire, the visual had thus changed, so also had the audible. The most remarkable alteration there is in the manner of reading. Augustine " comments on the fact—to him, apparently, remarkable—that Ambrose, when he read, read silently. You could see his eyes moving, but you could hear nothing. In such a passage one has the solemn privilege of being present at the birth of a new world. Behind us is that almost unimaginable period, so relentlessly objective that in it even ' reading ' (in our sense) did not yet exist. The book was still a *logos,* a speech; thinking was still *dialegesthai,* talking. Before us is our own world, the world of the printed or written page, and of the solitary reader who is accustomed to pass hours in the silent society of mental images evoked by written characters. This is a new light . . . on that turning inward. . . . It is the very moment of a transition more important, I would suggest, than any that is commonly recorded in our works of ' history.' "[1] It was " an outward and visible sign " of something that was happening, which Augustine himself was to develop, the surging interior distance, " the inward and spiritual grace " which was, for the Christian Church, the world of grace indeed. In that silent figure of Ambrose, it shut its mouth on the world.

It was, at the same time, opening its mouth in new sounds. Messias, so scholars say, uttered Aramaic. But when the Faith emerged into the Empire, it was speaking Greek. *Charis,* grace, was Greek; *agape,* love, was Greek; *tetalestai,* it is finished, was Greek. Yet Pentecost had already interfered and the Divine Spirit had been propagandist in many tongues. Its human missionaries followed that sublime example, and of all the languages they used, learned, modified, or enlarged, the greatest was Latin itself. The Faith had to talk Latin. The Mysteries were celebrated, it seems, both in Greek and Latin. The Sacred Books had been translated into Latin by the end of the second century. Tertullian at the same time made Africa " the Motherland of Christian Latin literature." By the end of the third century Jerome was collating

[1] *The Allegory of Love,* C. S. Lewis.

the Vulgate. The removal of the Court to Byzantium left the revival of Latin in the West unhampered, and what revived was the translated Latin of the Christian Church, assisted by the common talk of the common folk. The separation of languages opened another rift in the great imperial unity and did some harm to the unity of the Church itself, since meanings orthodox in the language of the West or the East easily became heretical in translation.

Literary Latin had always been something of a language apart, and the Church had not been anxious to encourage it. "I am a Christian," said Jerome in a dream to the heavenly host, and "no; you are a Ciceronian," they answered. Milton, when in *Paradise Regained* he rejected culture and the language of culture, was but following august predecessors. What the Church could not use, she tended to despise; "he that is not with me is against me." And literary Latin had hardly the scope that the Church needed. It could not, without altering itself, declare that Love could love, that Love could be loved, that our Yearning was crucified, that Another co-inhered in us and we in each other. Even the lovely and strange affections which move through what have been called the "elegancies" of Virgil had to cling eventually to the walls of his own Rome; they could not then find a greater air in another City. It was perhaps as much from an aesthetic as from a theological sense that Dante was bound to turn his great Master back from the Paradise of substitution. An ambiguity had entered into everything; grief was something besides grief, and joy besides joy. To say so is not to suggest that Christians, then or now, always felt or ought to have felt it so; it was not that they could not suffer or enjoy directly, but that a whole world of indirection had also been discovered. They might, contentedly and simply, sleep, eat, or make love. But once a week or so those simple satisfactions had the opportunity—and the duty—of seeing themselves illuminated by the Love that co-inhered in them.

The great Romantic religious movement therefore—the greatest of all Romantic movements—had opened, in literature as in life, before it knew what was happening. Other things went to help the great uprush of new sound which some immortal and aerial listener would have heard gradually rise from all the West of the Empire. " The aristocracy of Greek metres, with their delicate music of quantitative syllables, had maintained a precarious hold over Latin verse, the natural roots of which were fixed deep in the stressed peasant rhythms of threshing-flour, spinning-wheel, and country dance, the gnomic saws of the rustic oracle, and the heavy tramp of the marching legionary."[2] With the flight of Greek measures, these stresses returned. They were developed by littérateurs and poets, Christians or others, and also by Christians, poets or others. Ambrose revised the structure of verse. Augustine composed anti-heretical chants " for massed community sing-ing, with their rough scansion and shouting choruses. . . . Rhyme and assonance, features already familiar to folk-poetry, became prominent at the same time."[3] " Prudentius before the end of the fourth century turned the Ambrosian hymn into a Christian ode,[4] and introduced the cult of the martyrs into his verse, possibly with more devotion but with the same change of technique with which we recently introduced machines. Paulinus of Nola a little later composed the first Christian epithalamium[5] and in Gaul, before the year 600, Venantius Fortunatus had carried the new passion of the cross itself into verse when he composed the *Vexilla regis prodeunt*; or turned the march of the singing legions into the wholly new realism and adoration of the *Pange, lingua, gloriosi.* " My Eros is crucified "; the changed military tramp answered : *" dulce lignum, dulce clavo, dulce pondus sustinens."* Mystical and historical, the spaces of heaven and earth and all the movements of men circumambulated the Trophy.

It was this Christian and Catholic Empire—still in all ways one—which received continuously the impact and the infiltra-tion of the more barbarous races. The process was at first threefold. It consisted in the breakdown of the administration,

[2] *The Birth of the Middle Ages*, H. St. L. B. Moss.   [3] Ib.
[4] *Christian Latin Poetry*, F. J. E. Raby.   [5] Ib.

in the centripetal movements of the barbarians, and in the centrifugal movements of the Church. Almost as fast as the barbarians diluted and debased the receding frontiers of the Empire, the Church annexed and indoctrinated the advancing frontiers of the barbarians. The great pagan chieftains had to become Christians before they could become citizens, and it was citizens, though certainly patrician citizens, that most of them wanted to be. They had to accept the dogmas before they could display the lictors. They became, sometimes, the wrong kind of Christian; they accepted, sometimes, the wrong kind of dogma. The Arian heresy strengthened itself among the tribal princelings of Gaul and Germany, and the Catholic idea was assaulted in its metaphysical as well as its physical strongholds. But the philosophical discussion was, in fact, done; there also it was a war of frontiers. The energy of the Church thrust out into the wild as much as the hosts of the wild thrust into the civilized places. Boundaries of peoples, of cultures, of religions, melted in the pressure of multitudinous events.

The fact that the energy of the Christian Empire was the dominating force on one side produced one remarkable result. The civil administration in the West was in process of breaking down, as in the East it was in process of transformation. The senatorial and patrician houses lost their old Roman reputation. Civic office lost what attraction it had ever had. The priestly officers of the triumphant metaphysical idea took the place, to a very large extent, of the secular officers. There was no Navy, to speak of, in the West; law, owing to the mixture of various codes, was becoming unmanageable; the diplomatic service, as a separate entity, was practically non-existent. What could a young man of birth, who needed to take up a career, do? He could, of course, live quietly on his lands; he could go into commerce. He could try and attach himself to the provincial armies, which were sometimes imperial and sometimes anti-imperial. Or he could take orders and become, with luck, a dignitary.

It was not, certainly, as simple as that. Nor did it involve the choice of a safe, respectable, and wealthy career; on the contrary, it meant almost always the choice of a difficult, dangerous, and possibly deathly career. But Holy Orders were rapidly becoming not only the entrance to one career but almost the only entrance to any useful and progressive career at all. As a cleric, one might be sent anywhere to do anything; one controlled, fought, diplomatized, manipulated, exhorted, argued, converted. Careers had then, as always, to be found for sons—especially younger sons. The demands which, in quiet times, may reasonably be made upon ordinands —that they should be aware of a special vocation—were less urgent, though they remained urgent, than the demand that they should be intelligent and combative organizers both in the Church and in the cities. Unexpected—and unexpecting —laymen found themselves by popular clamour or clerical choice elected to the episcopate—Ambrose, Synesius, Sidonius. They protested; *nolo episcopari* was a heart-felt sentence then. They made conditions. Their conditions were accepted or they came under the compulsion of the local need. The priests were violently driven into secular functions and the laity were violently dragged into the priesthood. Before the Middle Ages were formed a great mass of tradition of a hierarchy saving the good things of this world, of ecclesiastics in lay administration, already existed. Gregory the Great was called in his epitaph " God's Consul." It is a notable title and it explains a great deal of the subsequent history of the Papacy and of the later Empire; the lay magistracy had to recover its business from the ecclesiastical organization to which it had of necessity been committed.

Nevertheless it may perhaps be admitted that this need assisted the natural tendency of any organization to rival the fact which it is supposed to be organizing. It is the belief of the whole Christian Church that the Holy Spirit will never allow this tendency within it to succeed; " the gates of hell shall not prevail against it." Organized salvation was still engaged in propagating in the world the Fact which was the salvation; the missionaries pressed out with the

Gospel precisely as the parish priests baptized babies. Christendom moved outward in space as it attempted to move forward in time. There is no other institution which suffers from time so much as religion. At the moment when it is remotely possible that a whole generation might have learned something both of theory and practice, the learners and their learning are removed by death, and the Church is confronted with the necessity of beginning all over again. The whole labour of regenerating mankind has to begin again every thirty years or so. Yet in spite of all its temptations and difficulties Christendom had really achieved a nature. It had begun under four conditions—Jewish nationality, Greek culture, Roman order, and human sin. It had reversed the relations between itself and the Jews, though it had not really made them much easier. Judaism now was as much like a Christian heresy as Christianity had originally been like a Jewish. Christendom had annexed and transformed a great number of Greek ideas, and it had denounced and banished others. It had re-organized and re-established the single Roman order into a double order, a two-faced, an ambiguous order, based again on co-inherence, for the other world certainly co-inhered in this, and this co-inhered in the other. That this relation had to be expressed in terms of time did not alter the fact that the relation was, properly, a thing including time. Messias had not returned visibly; his original Coming was farther and farther away. The Church, with extreme intelligence, had developed, largely through the assistance of Paul and Augustine, a doctrine which incidentally explained any apparent failure on its own part, the doctrine of the Fall of Man. Adam had not played a great part among the Jews; they had preferred Abraham. But the Christian doctors had recovered Adam; they expanded the most comfortable idea of the corruption of men's nature, and the free redemption which could, body and soul, correct it. But, redemption or no, concord or no, belief or no, time did co-inhere in eternity, and every single fact of time had to be answered for in eternity; that was what the co-inherence involved. "You shall give account for every idle word" was a mere philosophical fact, not a moral threat alone—not, indeed, a moral threat at all, for Messias himself would account in all who desired, by his infinite mercy separating things that were tares from things that were wheat.

Through all those centuries of clashing and changing frontiers, Christendom in terms of time and space extended itself. Its missionaries succeeded among the barbaric as they had among the cultured, and such gatherings as the Synod of Whitby, far by the North Sea and almost on the edge of the ancient Empire, repeated, to their degree, the Council of Nicaea. Both the Gospel and the Creed mastered the new world. But the method of conversion had perhaps changed somewhat. In the old days it had been individuals who had been converted, either by intellectual persuasion or spiritual violence, by grace, by intellect, or (at lowest) by fashion. But now it was whole communities which were abruptly annexed. The prestige, the power, and no doubt sometimes the piety of Christendom subdued one dynasty after another; a sudden rain of culture and Christianity descended over their territories, and the Christianity was often no more than the chief interference of the culture. The mass of the converts followed their lords into the territory of the spiritual City as into that of the temporal. Their loyalty to their chieftains no doubt contributed to that result; it was by no means a tyrannic compulsion but an almost "democratic" fidelity that governed them, nor was the reception of the Faith always subservient; it must have had about it at times something of the Jew accepting European tradition. But often it was imposed after defeat, though sometimes it was accepted after victory. Either way there were what may be called mass-conversions, and therefore uninstructed conversions. This is not to say they were insincere. But the crowds of husbandmen, sailors, and warriors could hardly be taught the philosophy of the Faith before baptism, nor could the majority, in all probability, be convinced of the Augustinian situation, of their need for the Redeemer, or of the presence of the Redeemer. A certain firmness came into action on the part of the great missionaries; they tended to say, as has so often been said about other states: " Love will come afterwards." The hierarchical complex of the Faith swept down over those intruding frontiers, over the supernatural fantasies, the natural loyalties, and the universal tragedy. It belonged, inevitably, to the Christian priesthood to encourage the vitality of the new religion, Martin of Tours, Cedd in Essex, Wilfrid in Northumbria. The subordinate masses were not left, as Christians under Islam were left, to work and to pay. Except (and even) in the case of the Jews, Christianity intended nothing less than an organic change. It proposed always to generate the world anew. It still deprecated violence. But its royal and lay misssionaries were not so conformable. Olaf swept up through Norway and Charlemagne out over Saxony; Alfred compelled the Danes to conversion. They saw before them cannibalism and wizardry and fate, and their honest but rash minds determined to end, by one means or another, the perils of supernatural evil. There was much to be said on their behalf; it was perhaps the only action possible to them. But the method had its disadvantages.

In fact, it is doubtful whether Christendom has ever quite recovered from the mass-conversion of the fashionable classes inside Rome and of the barbaric races outside Rome. Those conversions prepared the way for the Church of the Middle Ages, but the forcibleness of the conversions also prepared the way for the Church of all the after ages. It is at least arguable that the Christian Church will have to return to a pre-Constantine state before she can properly recover the ground she too quickly won. Her victories, among other disadvantages, produced in her children a great tendency to be aware of evil rather than of sin, meaning by evil the wickedness done by others, by sin the wickedness done by oneself. The actuality of evil does not altogether excuse the hectic and hysterical attention paid to it; especially to those who appear to be deriving benefit from it; especially to benefits which the Christian spectator strongly disapproves or strongly desires. Even contrition for sin is apt to encourage a not quite charitable wish that other people should exhibit a similar contrition. To grow into the vibrant web of universal and supernatural co-inherence is as difficult as to invite the direct and particular co-inherence of Almighty God. The natural mass is not the supernatural web—not even when it calls itself Christendom. If in the first energy of the young Church that fresh love had failed as often as the Epistles of St. Paul suggest, what was likely to happen when the masses were annexed to the later Church? The answer, it seems likely, is that *we* were, and in fact we have. We are still the mass; we are not very much like a web. Yet it cannot be supposed that any other method, had one been possible, would have produced a happier result. There was, after all, an alteration of attention. There was a difference between the Eucharist and human sacrifice. There was a difference between self-sacrificed and un-self-sacrificed Deity; between the God who died of His own will for the salvation of men and the God who died at others' will for the reproductiveness of vegetables. The attention given might, for long, be of the same quality as before, but the object of attention did in fact affect it—at any rate as far as to produce in many a moment of what was almost decision. The rites of sorcery which, it was believed, were practised had not, as their single, if remote, aim, the creation of a new will towards love; the new Christian rites had no other essential aim. Finally, the sense of heroic and utter despair which hovered, it seems, in the hearts of men and the genius of the poets, existed thereafter in the presence of a profound contrariety, as it does still. It was highly defined to be, at best, a mood, and at worst, sin. The whole tendency of human life and human thought was thus radically contradicted. This contradiction, welcome or unwelcome, was imposed on the mass. Christendom laboured under its converts; they seized, coloured, and almost ruined it. But they never changed the great metaphysical banners that floated over it; they never touched the Definitions. The Gospels may have been neglected but the Creed never failed.

Of the documents which survive from that period, two or three represent the change—the *Consolations of Philosophy* of Boethius, and the northern poems of *Beowulf* and the *Dream of the Rood*. The first was written by a Roman patrician and twice consul, imprisoned on charges of conspiracy by Theodoric the Ostrogoth (and Arian) when he dominated Italy. It became one of the great books of the Middle Ages; it was translated into English by King Alfred, Chaucer, and Queen Elizabeth, and it is still capable of being read as the work of a man teaching himself to *believe*. It is a high example of the thing that is bound to happen before the mass can become the web; though it is not formally Christian, it is Christ. Boethius has of course " believed "; and presently he is in prison, and the Lady Philosophy comes and asks him why he is so unhappy : " Art thou not the man that was taught and nourished in my school?"[6] It is this which drives the Roman back upon his self-examination. What is he? " I know that I belong to living men, intelligent, yet doomed to die." He confesses also that he knows that " Everything comes from God." These two sentences, however, represent, one might say, two different *kinds* of knowledge; the great question is whether the second answer can be known as the first is—" felt in the blood and felt along the heart." The argument proceeds along lines that were known indeed to pre-Christians, to Jews and to Greeks, as well as to Christians, but the Christian mind had been compelled to define them even more sharply. And King Alfred—he who was also in his day made by the Pope a consul of Rome— making his version for his people, did in fact so define them; he added such phrases as " But heavenly things naturally belong to thee, not earthly ones," and " the Way is God," and " But

[6] The quotations are from King Alfred's version, translated by W. J. Sedgfield.

I say, as do all Christian men, that it is a divine purpose that rules them, not Fate." There was no way of eluding the result, nor did the imprisoned Roman elude it; he followed his meditations to their only end—" Then all fortune is good." " Every lot is good . . . whether be it harsh or be it pleasing." So Philosophy; and Boethius: " At this I was afraid, and said: ' What thou sayest is true; yet I know not who would dare to say so to foolish men, for no fool could believe it."

This is the outer epigram, as it were, of the inner: " My Eros is crucified." It was quite different from the old Stoic tolerance of things as indifferent to the wise man; this is the first spark of the fire of charity and joy. It was another form of conversion, and it was precisely conversion that was, by the pressure of events, compelled to be an external rather than an interior thing. The world of the north turned, as the world of the south had done. *Beowulf* looks back on a pagan past; fatal existence, of gods and men, surrounded and bound to be defeated by monsters of the dark: " all glory ends in night." And though the doctrines changed, and the darkness of mortality became the infinite distance of immortality, the temper of the north for long remained. *" The Dream of the Rood* is a vision, in which the Gospel history of the Crucifixion is so translated that nothing is left except the devotion of the young hero (as he is called) and the glory; it is not acted on any historical scene, but in some spiritual place where there is no distinction between the Passion and the Triumph."[7] Indeed, the Passion had been the Triumph; the very Resurrection itself had begun before the darkness lightened and men were relieved of spiritual death.

Christendom itself had found another place of propaganda, almost (humanly) of genesis. Beyond the Empire, a land of law and culture, Ireland, had received the Gospel—some say, from the East; some, from immigrants escaping from Gaul: all say, from Patrick—and had become impregnated with the fire of our Lord the Spirit. St. Bridget assisted at the

[7] *English Literature, Medieval,* W. P. Ker.

Nativity; St. Colman called down angels to run races for his monks who could not go to the high feast. As the situation in what had been the West of the Empire became worse, and the far Byzantine government was more and more concerned with its immediate perils, the Irish saints renewed from the extremity of the world, where the Roman legions had never passed, a Pentecost of missions. Columcille reached Iona in 563; in 635 " the first cross of the English borderland was set up by men from Iona on a heathen moorland called the Heaven-field, by the ramparts of the Roman Wall."[8] At Lindisfarne, in Gaul, in Switzerland, in Italy, the Irish monks settled; Columban came to Rome and Gregory, " God's consul," received him; the high tides of Christendom met.

The Irish missionaries were mostly monks; another aspect of the same vocation had settled the south with convents. The countries over which the wars of the frontiers raged were colonized by religion. Egypt had yielded another kind of corn than that which of old had reached the Roman markets. The living ears of that growth had spread over the East, and Basil the Great there made a Rule for their future which, it is said, before he died in 379 had been accepted by eighty thousand monks. In the west they had floated on to the island of Lerins, just off the Riviera, where a group of ascetics followed their Way soon after 400. Their habit and reputation spread, and some century or so later, one who had also been a solitary in Italy made the first great Rule for the West; Benedict founded the monastery of Monte Cassino. He modified the extreme austerities; he reconciled even the monk to a life in time; he discouraged fantasies; he taught peace. He pledged his brethren to remain in the abbey of their situations, and he pledged the half-savage emulation of individual eccentricity to the decent obedience of holy order. He too taught the rule of co-inherence after a particular manner; the brethren were to know none but Christ in each other and in all. The Rule spread; it met and overcame the harsher Rule of Columban, and the most dedicated of lives rooted them-

[8] *Irish Nationality*, Mrs. J. R. Green.

selves in localities and in quiet. It was the frontier of Christendom which held most stable through all the terrible centuries.

Benedict died about the year 550; Columban in 615. A little before his death there came a night when, if the later chronicles of another people are to be believed, the crosses on all the churches in Byzantium began to sway, bloody lances luridly shone from a sky without a moon, the sacred Emperor was troubled in his sleep, and two monstrous creatures crawled out of the Nile. It was the night when in Mecca an archangel cried to Mohammed ibn 'Abdullah, ibn Abdalmuttalib, ibn Hashim, of the tribe of the Quraish, "Go; begin to preach."[9] Whether the crosses swayed or not, they might well have done, if material things can feel anything of their future, if there is any communication between age and age.

The Prophet was about forty-three years old; he had been converted to the One God some three years; he had almost a score of disciples. His activity began the next day, and it continued. In the year 628 an Arab messenger entered Jerusalem where the Eastern Emperor Heraclius then was and presented a letter signed "Mohammed, Messenger of God," bidding him abandon his beliefs and confess the Resignation. In the year 630 the first Army of the Resignation and of the Unincarnate Alone, offered battle to the central City of the Co-inherent and Incarnate. By 642 the whole Persian Empire had fallen, and Syria, and Palestine, and Egypt. The Patriarchates of Antioch, of Jerusalem, of Alexandria, lay under the green banner of Islam, and the Throne and Patriarchate of Byzantium were threatened by it from across the narrow seas. By 695 the rest of northern Africa had gone, so completely that it is difficult now to remember that once it held great provinces of Rome, and that Augustine, Cyprian, Tertullian, Clement, and Origen, though they thought of themselves as loyal in every fibre of their being to the European City, lived in and shaped the thought of Christian Europe from Africa. The most opposite earthly frontier of Christen-

[9] *Mohammed*, Essad Bey.

dom had been drawn, both in military and metaphysical affairs. Christendom was, and remains, for all its victories, in a state of siege. Byzantium then, like London to-day, found itself on the edge of the war; it almost fell in 717. Spain did fall in 711; the south of Gaul was almost occupied by 732. The Emperor Leo III in the East and Clovis the King of the Franks in the West separately defeated Islam, and the great cavalry charges were checked. The frontier lay, uncertain and vibrating, south of the Pyrenees, along the coast of Africa, up the coast of Asia, inward around Asia Minor (the last precarious bastion of the Empire on the opposite side of the Golden Horn), and along the Caucasus to the Persian Sea. Locked in a strange debate among those last fabulous hills, the two Powers contended for the doctrine of the soul.

In days when most things were spoken of in terms of the soul, this propinquity had one marked if accidental effect; it tautened awareness of false doctrine within, especially the awareness of the Jews. Jews and Mohammedans might disagree about Mohammed. But they equally rejected not merely the Gospel of Christ but the very Nature of Christ. The growing devotion to the Mother of God was an abomination to both; the intense complex of the union of Manhood—that is, of matter—and of Godhead was an outrage to both, and to the awful Otherness of Deity in which they both believed. No doubt Jew, Mohammedan, and Christian could live comfortably enough together, so long as nothing happened. But the least sneer—and the fires and the massacres might everywhere begin. The mass-conversion of Christians and of Mohammedans, the racial self-centredness of the Jews, offered for centuries a dangerous material. The finished and finite clods of the three Creeds might be untroubled by heavenly sparks; they were prone to be lit by earthly.

Of that underlying contention a sign, if not a result, was the appearance of a schism in Christendom itself, the coming of the iconoclasts, of the image-breakers. In the same decade decrees were issued against all images by the Khalif of Islam in his dominions and by his enemy the Emperor Leo in his.

The miraculous image of Christ was removed by a soldier from the Bronze Gate of the Hall of the Imperial Palace; a crowd, mostly of women, upset his ladder and beat him to death with clubs. It was asserted that, by such an attack on representations of the Divine Flesh and Its Mother, the Emperor and his friends were denying the Incarnation; it was answered that because of the uniqueness of that Flesh representations were impermissible. "The image is the symbol of Christ," said St. John Damascene; "the honour paid to the image passes to its prototype," said St. Basil. "No image can depict the Two Natures," answered their opponents; "every image is therefore heretical. His only proper representation is in the Eucharist which is He." In fact the controversy was not only philosophical; it was also psychological. Is there a point at which idolatry tends to begin? a point at which the attention paid to the Person begins to be paid to the Representation, at which fervour begins to aim at the image instead of the idea? All the purer consciousness of man answered that there was. It had been found by experience to be so, and the Bishop of Marseilles had had statues in his diocese broken because of it. Ought not the danger then to be removed? The common sense of Christendom refused that solution; the purer consciences would have to make the best of the bad job that humanity undoubtedly was. The Byzantine and Roman Patriarchs were at one; the monks and the women supported them. The Emperor Constantine V pursued his father's policy; he summoned a gathering of over three hundred bishops who declared against images; he sent his soldiers against the monks; but from the secret chambers of the palace his wife Irene (the daughter of an Eastern Khan) supported the icons. The icons—such of them as were miraculous—did their best to support their own cause; dreadful things happened by their outraged power. The Popes refused any longer to obtain sanction of the Emperor for their consecration; the East and the West divided under the strain. Constantine died; Irene in the name of her young son seized the Government, and through a new

Patriarch caused a new Council to be called. Legates from the Pope attended. The earlier gathering was stigmatized as a " judaizing Sanhedrin " and the later restored the images. The Council issued its decrees for all Christendom in 786. The Empress Irene, having established the propriety of doing honour to the prototype through the image, proceeded to establish her own honour by deposing, blinding, and imprisoning her son the Emperor. But though she had suppressed iconoclasm through her reign—till 802—it broke out later; and only when in 842 another Empress on the—natural—death of her son found herself in power did the quarrel cease with the final restoration of images. A great procession through Byzantium, in which the Empress walked, re-established them on a Festival still kept by the Greek Church as the Feast of Orthodoxy. It was for centuries accepted in Christendom (in spite of a reluctance on the part of Charlemagne to promulgate the decision of 786 in the West) that the Affirmation of those actual images was good and just. Men must use their piety and intelligence to avoid idolatry; they could not and must not be saved by the Rejection of Images, except as their private vocations might dictate. But private vocations are not to lay down the law to Christendom; images —one may add, living images also—were to receive " proskunesis," particular honour. The frontier was determined.

Meanwhile in the West other shapes had begun to emerge, forms of the first half-fabulous Christian kings. They appear for a little, and then perhaps their dynasties fail, and we lose sight of their brief cultures; they are separated perhaps by a century or so, but they appear; just as, a little later, the cities of Italy begin to loom again with their magistrates; or as the universities are suddenly discovered to have come into being, and our attention is distracted from William Rufus or the First Crusade by the voice of Abelard lecturing at Paris. But the kings are the earlier, and the greatest of the kings is Charlemagne. In the frost and snow of a Frankish winter, a boy of twelve, he first appears to us meeting the Pope Stephen II who had come from Rome to ask Pepin the Frank for help against the Lombards. Pepin consented; he defeated the enemy; he took twenty-one cities from them and gave them to the Pope, and withdrew again across the Alps. Twelve years later his son Charles succeeded him, with a mind already formed to achieve three purposes of power—military power to crush his enemies, religious power to direct souls, intellectual power to instruct both souls and minds. These, by himself or his servants, he proposed and proceeded to accomplish. He founded Society. " In him that which had been unformed and inarticulate achieved shape and lucidity, and the large framework of Christian Europe was focused and stood out clearly before men."[10] It was determined by him (more than by any other one man except Gregory the Great) that the new political order should at its best be, and at its worst pretend to be, Christian for a thousand years. But it was also determined because of him if not by him—we cannot tell—that the new political order should be independent both of the old Imperial order and of the new ecclesiastical. There had been, since Augustus, many revolts in the provinces against the central Roman Government. The legions of Gaul and of Britain, of Pannonia and Syria, had often enough elected and acclaimed an Emperor. Constantine himself had come to Rome, and therefore to Byzantium, through something very much like a revolt. But now the applauding legions were to be not military but clerical; the ecclesiastical forces of the West chose an Emperor. It was no new thing, and yet it was a very new thing. There was no immediate intention to substitute the chosen figure for the ruler at Byzantium; but the very Coronation implied a substitution. On Christmas Day in the year 800 the thing was done.

In St. Peter's at Rome the Pope sang Mass. The King of the Franks knelt there, clothed out of courtesy in the Roman manner. The Pope sang the last phrase of the Rite; after private prayer the King was about to rise; he saw the Pope descending towards him; he paused. The Pope set a crown on his head, and called out, and all the great congregation

[10] *Charlemagne,* Douglas Woodruff.

shouted after him : "Life and victory to Charles Augustus, crowned after God's will, mighty and peace-giving Emperor!" The Pope prostrated himself. Where the King of the Franks had come in, the Emperor departed.

He said afterwards that he did not know it had been planned. But he lived up to it. He wrote in his dispatches : "Charles, by the will of God, Roman Emperor, Augustus . . . in the year of Our consulship I." He had an oath taken to him as Cæsar by all officers, lay or ecclesiastical. He sent ambassadors to soothe the anger of Byzantium; in 812 the Eastern court acknowledged him. Yet as in old times the Emperor elected by the legions had particularly to appease and satisfy (or to subdue) the legions, so for after-centuries the new Emperors had to satisfy (or to subdue) the ecclesiastical power which had appointed them. "By the will of God—" but directly? or by mediation of the Bishop of Rome? The forms, personal or documentary, were new, but the quarrel was very very old.

The renewal of the Imperial dignity in the West did nothing to reconcile the tendency to schism between the East and the West; if anything, it accelerated its movement. It was already long since the Church of Rome had come to regard itself, and to be regarded, as the protector of orthodoxy. "From the very first the Roman Church had seized, as by a creative intuition, on the idea of Order as the basis of the universe. . . . But the spiritual presentation of the theory came not from Europe, but from Africa. . . . The laying of the spiritual foundation is represented by Tertullian; the raising of the ecclesiastical framework by Cyprian; the consolidation and completion of the entire edifice by Augustine."[11]

The missionary energy of the Popes had decreed the advance of that order; settlements and churches were absorbed into it. But the solidarity of such an ecclesiastical movement in the West failed before the equally ancient, equally learned, equally determined, and equally devout tradition of the East. The sacerdotal glory of the Sacred Emperor presented an even more

[11] *Literary History of the Early Church,* Cruttwell.

symbolical expression of the mystical union of Christendom with God than did the Supreme Pontiff on the Caelian hill. Languages accentuated differences and raised suspicion of heresies; a whole distinction between cultures exposed itself, and while the speculative meditations of the East fastened on the Incarnation, the more legal attention of the West disputed over the Atonement. There were already all the fissiparous elements which create a frontier.

As is the habit in these periods of division, a number of quarrels broke out at once. Normal developments and unfortunate (but not unusual) incidents—frontier incidents—were challenged. The doctrinal incident was perhaps the most serious, as it was in some sense the most negligible. The sacred Nature of our Lord the Spirit had been long since defined to proceed from the Father; it was universally accepted. It was all but universally accepted that He also proceeded from the Son. But the phrase so defining it had not been included in the final formation of the Creed, and Oecumenical Councils had decreed that there should be no addition made to the Creed. The ardour of a Council in Spain (whose fervour has so often been inconvenient to Europe!) defended the Deity of the Son against some unorthodox teaching by declaring that any who denied the Procession from the Son should be anathema. He from whom God proceeded must himself be God. The devout and orthodox Spaniards began to sing *Filioque* in the Creed, and the habit spread. Charlemagne adopted it for the royal chapel at Aix, and so through his dominions. The Pope Leo, who had had the original Creed inscribed on silver plates in Greek and Latin and set up in St. Peter's, refused to adopt it. But the thing had happened, and the East, as orthodox as Spain, heard with horror a revised and expanded Creed used through the West. The offence grew greater still when it was known that at last the Roman See, when occupied by Nicholas I, had consented to ratify the interpolation.

But if there was a verbal interpolation in the West there

was an interpolation of a different kind in Byzantium. The Sacred Emperor, having committed incest, had been refused communion by the Patriarch. For this and other offences the Patriarch was deposed, and a learned layman Photius compulsorily ordained and imposed in the See. He announced his election to the Pope, to whom the original Patriarch Ignatius also appealed. The Pope sent legates who at a Council (he said) " betrayed him " and agreed to the deposition. The angry arguments went on. Photius in 876 denounced the West in eight articles, but the Sacred Emperor was murdered in that year and Photius himself was deposed.

It has been said that " it is difficult to know whether Photius or Ignatius was the more badly treated." Causes of offence between the East and the West multiplied, and a territorial dispute was added to the theological and the ecclesiastical. There was a high diplomatic wrangle whether Bulgaria should be joined to the Axis of the Eastern Patriarchates or to the single autocratic government of Rome. The Balkans and Spain, one way or another, distract Europe continually. An uneasy peace settled down for two centuries; then suddenly Michael Cerularius, Patriarch of Constantinople, provoked the storm. He accused the West of heresy; he closed the churches of the Latin rite. The Popes asserted the orthodoxy of the West and the primacy of Rome; they maintained open in Italy the churches of the Byzantine rite. The Patriarch removed the name of the Pope from the prayers. The Papal legates, entering the Church of the Holy Wisdom in Byzantium, just before the celebration of the Divine Liturgy, ascended through the crowd to the altar, and laid on it the solemn excommunication of the Patriarch and all his followers from the co-inherence of their Christendom. The frontier of a thousand years was drawn on 16th July, 1054.

CHAPTER V

THE IMPOSITION OF BELIEF

By the eleventh century the wars of the frontiers were drawing slowly to an end. Both mentally and corporally they would be continued through the Middle Ages, but then they would be on the frontiers of an established secular thing, the massive body of Christendom, stretching from the Black Sea to Ireland and from Scandinavia to Aragon. Messias had not, even now, returned; and the expectation of his coming had changed. Interior illuminations were discouraged. Exteriorly, the Second Coming had turned into something similar yet different; through all those converted masses it was presented now as the Day of Judgment. The success of Christendom very properly checked itself with a recollection of its certain and dangerous end; Christ who was the judge became the Judge who was Christ. A catastrophe of hope and of terror threatened the world; but it threatened from afar, and (generally speaking) it threatened without the illumination which, in the early days of the Church, touched the catastrophe with joy. It was admitted that the Two Cities with which Augustine had encouraged the Christians of his day—the City that was of God and the City that was not of God—had grown intermingled again and would have to be separated. *Dies irae, dies illa . . .* Even Bede had supposed himself to be living in the last age of the world, and with the near approach of the year one thousand of the Fructiferous Incarnation the eyes of Christendom everywhere expected the end.

It did not come. The first millennium of Christendom closed and the second opened with no greater terror than the ordinary robberies, murders, rapes, burnings, wars, massacres, and plagues, and the even less noticeable agonies of each man's ordinary life. But some lessening in these, some quiescence of anarchy, some stability, began to be generally discernible. The new age has its beginnings signalized by the rise of the Universities, and the reason is that men began again to have time to talk, to argue, and to think. There began again to be places where, more or less undisturbed, they could do so. And finally, there began again to be reasonably easy possibilities of transport. Men could pass from town to town; the schools could communicate. Talking and thinking had gone on for the past six hundred years, but they had been very much *ad hoc,* though the *hoc* had differed. It might be the *Filioque* clause; it might be the scandals caused by Pope Sergius III and his mistress Marizia or Pope Anastasius III and his mother the same Marizia; it might be, more usually, the nearness or distance of hostile armies—" what the Greek intends and what the Frank." But now men began at last to be less aware of immediate loss and immediate gain. They had time for the speculative intellect, and for the organization of the speculative intellect. The grand metaphysical civilization began to establish itself on its two stable elements—dogma and the land. All the rest was administration.

On the social and economic side, the material was the land, the form was tenure, and the defining virtue was loyalty. This is not to say that loyalty was always very noticeable. But in order that it should be defined, or that disloyalty should be excused, there developed a complicated legal system. In the *Comedy* of Dante, the worst sinners are those who have betrayed their lords and benefactors, and the feudal breach of honour of which Judas is guilty corresponds to the spiritual schism provoked by Brutus and Cassius. The phrases may be interchanged so because the Middle Ages were not split into two entities called Church and State— or not, at any rate, as much as our own age has till recently been. Christendom was dealing on one side with temporal and on the other with eternal affairs, but it was one Christendom, and time and eternity were still both co-inherent. The Pope was a temporal lord, as were the bishops; the Emperor was a spiritual officer, as were his lords. Society found a form into which it could grow, just as the intellect found a means by which it could operate. The organization of grace set to work, as it were, to catch up with time and space, to baptize and convert the too-quickly succeeding generations of the mass into the holy vision of co-inherence through the Salvation. The martyrs, the saints, and the Mother of God (" *figlia del tuo figlio* ") prolonged the vision to " the topmost reaches of our human wit." Men were to be made into lovers; the world had another opportunity to be generated anew.

But the single aim of the double operation could not always reconcile the double executives. Long before, when the Church rejected Gnosticism, and again when confessors as such were refused the sacerdotal dignity, it had been laid down that the priestly offices of regeneration were not, in themselves, supposed to be better or purer than anyone else. This view the laity, especially the lay officers, very strongly took, at the same time that they developed an equally strong tendency to demand that the priesthood should precisely be better and purer than anyone else. It would have been (humanly speaking) almost impossible for the clergy to have been as good as the lay hierarchy demanded, nor did they, as a whole, make the effort. They were content to occupy their undoubtedly advantageous position, which consisted quite simply in the fact that while the clergy could do everything that the laity could do, the laity could not do everything that the clergy could do. And by definition the particular preroga- tives of the clergy were, in the last resort, the more important. It is true that the sacramental system was not then quite so strictly reserved to the clergy as it has been since the end of the Middle Ages. In the hour of danger of death laymen could absolve each other and could even do something very like celebrating Mass. But such possibilities were not normal, and the normal clerical advantages were often, as in other periods, the cause of anti-clerical irritations. The irritation was cer- tainly wrong, though the anti-clericalism was probably right. It is part of the price the priesthood pay for their vocation—

just as, if ever poets were to become the acknowledged legislators of the world, a strong anti-poetic movement would have to be encouraged. But then also the vocation of the poets, as of the priesthood, must be respected. The nervous strain which developed at that time exhibited itself most spectacularly in the struggle between the Emperor and the Pope. Since time depended on eternity, the papal party were to hold that the Emperor depended on the Pope. But since also time is at present autonomous the Imperial party held that the Emperor was independent of the Pope; and if the Pope forgot or neglected his eternal office in time, the Emperor, precisely by virtue of his temporal suzerainty, might even correct, chastise, or control the Pope. It was this quarrel between two modes of existence which affected all the relations between the lay and clerical hierarchies everywhere.

But this was within the Christian civilization of which all approved. There were greater questions; there was the matter of the protection of that civilization. The cause of its rise had been the expansion of doctrine; the basis of its continuation was understood as doctrine; its preservation therefore meant the defence of doctrine. During the Dark Ages that doctrine had tended, one way and another, to accumulate certain accretions, of which one was the devil and his angels. The devil had not, in the early days of Christendom, been of quite so much importance as he had since become. There is certainly no rational argument against him; there is perhaps a psychological, for something very much like dualism is apt to follow the devil, and in fact dualism did re-appear in the Middle Ages. He had a long tradition behind him; he had a dubious existence in the Jewish myths of Samael the Accursed, and the pagan deities of the Mediterranean or of the northern forests had helped to materialize him. He had crept into Greek philosophy. " Hellenism knew of no anti-gods." But " Plato, towards the end of his life, was supposed to have dallied with the idea of an evil world-soul; Plutarch adopted it more decidedly."[1] The Church, having formally subdued

[1] *Plotinus,* W. R. Inge.

the anti-good to the good, had compensated it by giving it practically a free hand in its own domains. Theories of the Atonement accentuated the devil's existence by giving him a right to man's soul, which necessitated the shedding of the Precious Blood as a legal ransom. A kind of belated and popularized Gnosticism was allied with a romantic melodrama, and man was at the same time a little excused for his original error and provided with an ever-contemporary subject for moral reprobation.

The operations of the devil, besides the general temptations proper to the flesh and soul, consisted particularly of provocations to witchcraft and to heresy. Of the two, the second was the more usual. Witchcraft flourished, like crime, at certain times and at certain places; and at some, unduly. But it was never either so universal as heresy or as disease. It was, under examination, as difficult to be quite orthodox as to be quite healthy. Yet the need of orthodoxy, like the need of health, was imperative; the danger of epidemics was serious and regarded seriously. The Middle Ages were the great scientific and medical age of Europe; only their science, like their medicine, was of the soul. The bestiaries and the hagiologies were like our own popular scientific works; they " wrote down " to the crowd, but what they wrote down were always the same principles as were more accurately expressed by the great theologians. In the same way heresy was not only metaphysical but psychological; the heresiarchs, like the saints, were the psycho-analysts of the time. Heresy was not only a matter of belief concerning the nature of Super-Essential Love, which of course it was, but also a matter of how men were to love, how they were to co-inhere, how in fact they did co-inhere. It was many centuries since the ecclesiastical authorities had first invoked the secular power. Nor were they now in any hurry to do so. The unorthodox at first were more apt to be attacked by the crowd, and the clergy were usually called in, like the police, as much to save as to destroy them. But the police were soon in an impossible position; the magistrates had no code to work by.

Earnest magistrates and lax magistrates varied in their decisions. The whole matter needed to be regularized. In 1184 the Emperor Frederick Barbarossa and the Pope Lucius III promulgated the Edict of Verona. The Pope commanded the bishops to search out heresy, and to hand the guilty over to the secular power for punishment; the Emperor proclaimed punishment against them. It might almost be said that here the Church Militant underwent her most serious dangers, and that she deliberately accepted a mode of action difficult to reconcile realistically with the Kingdom towards which she aspired. It is true that heresy was believed seriously to harm man's capacity to live and to love; the heretic outraged the law and method of exchange—nay, by insisting on his view as against the authoritatively-expounded view of the Church he refused the common fact of supernatural exchange. It was perhaps bound to seem necessary that he should himself be cut off. " Life is the means by which man enters beatitude," and heresy spoiled it.

But, that being admitted, it is clear also that new temptations of the greatest energy were now assailing the organization. There has never yet been found any method of driving out one devil—except by pure love—which does not allow the entrance of seven, as Messias had long ago pointed out. With the establishment of the Inquisition in 1233, every kind of effort was made to drive out the one. The duty of delation was encouraged everywhere. " A boy of fourteen or a girl of twelve " were old enough to bear testimony. Not to do so was itself heresy, just as to complain of the Inquisition was heresy. The whole Inquisitorial Service was given a job by which the Means Test of to-day grows pale. It was a job in which they could hardly ever go wrong, and in which the accused were always at an incredible disadvantage. Convolutions of doctrine were far more dangerous than difficulties of fact. A man accused of heresy had generally been guilty of heresy. " Brother accused brother, wife husband." The Church committed herself, on the highest possible principles, to a breach of the highest possible principles. She did not merely execute; she caused to her prisoners, and she handed her prisoners over to, deliberate and prolonged torture, mental or physical or both. She approved the prolongation of that torture to its extreme point; she made any protest a matter of heresy. One would think that the phrase of Lord Acton (that " it cannot be held that in Rome sixteen centuries after Christ men did not know that murder was wrong ") might be held to apply; it cannot be that men did not think such methods doubtfully holy. It was not so. Deep, deeper than we believe, lie the roots of sin; it is in the good that they exist; it is in the good that they thrive and send up sap and produce the black fruit of hell. The peacock fans of holy and austere popes drove the ashes of burning men over Christendom. The torch that had set light to the crosses in the Vatican gardens of Nero did not now pass into helpless or hesitating hands.

All this development, however, took time, and other great movements ran parallel with it. When, by a most fortunate chance, William of Champeaux found peace enough to deliver at Paris a course of lectures on the text of Porphyry, the Middle Ages found themselves. Porphyry was a pagan, a neo-Platonist, an Alexandrian; a contemporary of Origen, and a disciple of Plotinus. The young intellectuals thronged to hear the lectures. In a world which depends on printed matter, it is odd to think how much of the greater developments in Christendom have come not by books but by lectures. The living voice directs and dominates, from Messias himself on to the Renascence, and again after the Renascence in sermons, and through our mechanical inventions we are turning back to the living voice to-day, when millions of households listen to their political masters and believe. Yet without the eye the thing is incomplete; the audiences of Paris heard not merely a voice, but the speech of a man.

With those lectures the University of Paris may be said to have begun; what made it sure was the work of William's opponent and successor Abelard. Abelard, like Origen, like Montaigne, is one of those figures of whom Christendom has never felt quite certain, and yet from whom Christendom has derived much energy. The outburst of intellect expressed one side of itself in him, as the other was expressed in his contemporary Anselm of Canterbury. The great problem, and the great excitement, for the early medieval minds was quite different from ours. We have the questions—say, *What is going on, if anything?* or *Does God exist?*—but no answers until we discover them, if we do. But even then we have no means of checking the answers. The Middle Ages supposed themselves to have both the questions and the answers. They had ordinary things on one hand; they had the highly technical language of ritual and doctrine on the other. What was the relation between the two? The excitement lay in pointing out that your opponents' arguments, if prolonged, would result in a denial of the formally correct answers with which he was supposed to concur. The excitement also, no doubt, sometimes lay in yourself using arguments which " made Truth look as near a lie As could comport with her Divinity." A legate from Rome in those early days is said to have written home to his lord protesting that it was indecent that young boys should be publicly arguing that God did not exist.

Credo ut intelligam, said Anselm, and defined the wiser method. *Intelligo ut credam,* Abelard almost said, and might have added *dubito ut credam.* At least the famous *Sic et Non,* a collection of contradictory passages in the Scriptures and Fathers which Abelard offered for reconciliation, stirred hostility. But that was as elementary as it was sincere; it was his developed rationalism, seeming to be too audacious, too negligent of the right doctrinal answers, which ruined Abelard. He came into collision with " the implacable fanaticism of the redoubtable St. Bernard."[2] St. Bernard composed the *Tractatus de erroribus Abaelardi,* and called into action the machinery of rebuke. " The inspired ignorance and unscrupulous astuteness of the saint procured a condemnation at the Council of

[2] *Legacy of the Middle Ages,* G. C. Crump and E. F. Jacob; *Philosophy,* C. R. S. Harris.

Sens, which did not even listen to a defence."[8] St. Bernard felt that sacred things, profound secrets such as " My Eros is crucified," were not meant to be the subjects of the juvenile analysis and presumptuous wrangles of the schools and the streets. But though he was victorious at the time, the influence of Abelard lasted, and the Church was saved from the silence imposed by holy men upon those of other temperaments. She had difficulties enough with the mystical experimentalists at best; it would have been intolerable that they should have refused to allow her the good of reason, and the good of dialectic, and even the good of doubt. " Let your conversation be Yea, yea, and Nay, nay," said Messias, and perhaps (more than we have thought) meant it to be both at once. But the saints would almost have ruled out the Nay—in that kind of conversation—altogether.

Dialectic proceeded. Abelard died in 1142; St. Thomas Aquinas began to lecture in 1252. But between them the great spectacular moment of the imposition of belief had already come into existence, and had already hardened. It was the Fourth Council of Lateran, convoked by Innocent III in 1215. There the exhibition which marks the triumph of organized Western Christendom existed; more than four hundred bishops, twice as many abbots and priors, and all kinds of representatives of the lay princes. It is true that it was a clerical assembly, but in matters of doctrine the power of decree (if not always the initiative of decree) had always lain with the priesthood. It is true also that it seems rather to have recorded the decisions of its Papal head than to have produced any discussions of its own. But as far as the imposition of the idea of Christendom upon the mass of mankind went, these characteristics do but heighten the effect. The personality and power of Innocent, and his success, image the Middle Ages; by a hundred years after Lateran the catastrophes which shook them are already in sight.

Lothair di Segni, called Innocent III, had ascended the Papal Throne in 1198. He had found Europe pressed by dangers both without and within—the Mohammedans in the Near East and the heretical Cathari in the south of France. He proposed an effort to overthrow both. The First Crusade against Islam had taken place in 1097-9, at the request of the Eastern Emperor, and under the impetus of Urban II. It had taken Jerusalem and created Latin kingdoms in the East. A hundred years afterwards, Saladin re-took Jerusalem, and the Third Crusade failed, in spite of the passion of Richard Cœur-de-Lion, to recover it. In 1202 the Fourth Crusade set out, under the encouragement of Innocent. It set out; it was diverted. The city of Byzantium lay always across the path of the Western armies. It was at once intimate and alien; their base, yet their rival; Christian, yet schismatic. Since the Separation of the Rites, it had become a provocation both to the creed and the greed of the West. In 1204 the temptation of its arrogance, its wealth, and its heresy proved too much. The Crusade was turned; on some dynastic excuse they first entered, and afterwards besieged, took, and sacked the City. It was the first great example of civil destructiveness within Christendom; the West, in that act, invited a violence of schism, as if Christendom, like the world, could no longer resist an interior cannibalism, and as if it there ignorantly prepared for itself the later disasters of its own Religious Wars. Obviously, we still suffer from that act and from the failure of the Crusades to-day; it is the loss of Byzantium which has allowed of the growth of Prussia and its effort to dominate the East. Innocent so far acceded as to accept what looked like the Greek overthrow, and to make a Venetian the Latin Patriarch of Byzantium.

In Languedoc older heresies than Islam had appeared—the Gnostic, the Manichæan. There, in the most highly civilized region of Europe, the city of Albi in Provence gave its name to the followers of those ancient schisms in natures, the thought of matter as incapable of salvation, the thought of the Perfect group of adepts. It is true that most of what we know of the Albigenses comes through their enemies, and that not one mind in a thousand can be trusted to state accurately what its opponent says, much less what he thinks. The orthodox testimony cannot be trusted more than, though perhaps it may be trusted as much as, that of anthropologists regarding savage races. It seems clear that Languedoc had become a centre of culture, of luxury, of heresy, and of sterility. A kind of " waft of death " went out there, and an oriental separation from the flesh and the co-inherence; the Eros was crowned, but it did not fructify. At first Innocent sent missionaries; the great Dominic sent himself. But the missionaries failed; the papal legate was murdered; and Innocent " proclaimed, for this invasion of Languedoc, all the indulgences that could be earned by the far more difficult and dangerous campaign in the Holy Land."[4] An army collected in France, led by Simon de Montfort, and advanced against the heretics. There were horrible cruelties, more than those habitual to war. At last the country was conquered; the doctrine was taught everywhere, and the domain passed from its original lords the Counts of Toulouse into the hands of the officially more Christian Kings of France. By 1215 the thing was finished, and the doctrine that matter was incapable of salvation was, until the coming of Mrs. Eddy, a fallacy of the past.

But among the advancing and delighted intellects, and among the efforts to direct and control the too easily converted masses, and among the hurrying of propagandists and persecutors, and the quarrels of the spiritual and secular hierarchies, there had all this while developed another affair of more importance than any. This also had to do with matter and with Man. The great definitions of the Trinity and of the Incarnate had, on the whole, been decided long before; Nicæa and Chalcedon had settled them. But in those earlier centuries the central Mystery of Ritual, the Eucharist itself, had rather been accepted than discussed. From the days of St. Paul the holy celebrations had continued, and the presence of Messias been acknowledged. But argument had

[4] *Inquisition and Liberty*, G. C. Coulton.

been small. The nature of the change had not been defined, nor had the means or moment of the change been settled.

Only the most subtle theologians can adequately discuss the Nature of that Presence. The taunts flung at the Church concerning her preoccupation with doctrine seem more justified here than in most places, as the confused lay mind toils to understand the material Body which is yet spiritual, or how the " accidents were in some sense real " and " it was by means of this distinction between substance and accidents . . . that St. Thomas and others could maintain that, while the species were really broken, the Body of Christ was not,"[5] and yet consubstantiation is doubtfully orthodox. The answers are lofty and sublime, but we yet await the genius who can make those high speculations vivid. What is certain is that there had been little controversy in the Church over these things, and it was not until in the late Middle Ages the habit of adoration tended, so far as the Commons of Christendom were concerned, to take the place of Communion. St. Ignatius had spoken of the Eucharist as " the flesh of our Saviour which suffered for our sins," and from those earliest days the eyes of Christendom had been fixed on the elements which, being the veil, were in some sense rather the mystery beyond. The identity of the substantial Sacrifice—that is, of the substituted surrender of Himself—was presented by God to man and by man to God; the great Rite soared to its climax in the eternal, and yet communicated the eternal to time—" terrible to speak of," wrote Fulbert of Chartres. Matter had been capable of salvation; salvation was communicated through matter. " In the very hour of the sacrifice . . ." wrote Gregory the Great, " things lowest are brought into communion with the highest, things earthly are united with the heavenly, and the things that are seen and those which are unseen become one."[6]

Innocent III had, before he was Pope, written a book on

[5] *The Council of Trent and Anglican Formularies,* H. Edward Symonds.

[6] *History of the Doctrine of the Eucharist,* Darwell Stone.

the Sacrament. When he had summoned the Council he caused it to open its decrees with a declaration " On the Catholic Faith." It ran :

" There is one universal Church of the faithful, outside which no one at all is in a state of salvation. In this Church Jesus Christ himself is both priest and sacrifice; and His body and blood are really contained in the sacrament of the altar under the species of bread and wine, the bread being transubstantiated into the body and the wine into the blood by the power of God, so that, to effect the mystery of unity, we ourselves receive of that which is His, what He himself received of that which is ours."

The last phrase is notable. As it were in a lyric of theology the doctrine of exchange, of substitution, of co-inherence reached its highest objective point on earth. History and contemporaneity and futurity were joined; the Church had been reconciled to time only to reconcile time to its Cause. It answered the judgment and terrible threat of heaven precisely with the ancient cry, itself transfigured : " My Eros is crucified "; it sank, it veiled itself, it almost dared to murmur : " Thy Eros is crucified." And at the same time it imposed that most tender and most awful secret upon all the children of the West, as the East also did, whatever variations of phraseology or hesitations over ritual occurred between them.

It was about this time that the whole subject was in literature raised into a kind of different power. Someone, of course, did it, but he is as unknown to us as that other who altered the whole future of the drama by first having a religious play performed outside the church. That certainly may have been done in several places almost at once, but certainly someone made the vocal suggestion first, and even more certainly some one person invented Galahad. The great Arthurian romances had grown up and spread during the twelfth and early thirteenth centuries. The energy of courtly love had gone into Lancelot, Merlin had come into existence, and so had the grand myth of the Grail and the Wounded King. It is supposed that a Cistercian or a group of Cistercians set to work both to concentrate and to undo the cycle of the Matter of Britain. There was built up, in the romances called the *Lancelot* and the *Queste del Saint Graal,* a world of chivalry and love in order to be overthrown by the creation of another world of religion, contrition and sanctity; and as in that world the Grail shone defined, the same as and yet (in effect) other than the Eucharist, so in proportion to its pure glory Lancelot was barred from achieving it. But by what has been one of the greatest moments of imagination ever permitted to man, he was allowed and compelled, in an enchantment and supposing himself true to the queen, to beget on the predestined mother the shape of the High Prince. Galahad, accompanied by Percivale and Bohort (as if in different offices of a single sanctity), achieves the Grail. No doubt, at that time, Galahad presented, as it were, the Way of Rejection of Images as against the mistaken or sinful affirmations of images in the court of Camelot. But there is—to us, especially since Malory —a great ambiguity about him. He has no concern with any mortal affirmations, and yet he is the child and climax of the greatest of mortal affirmations, of a passionate, devout, and tragic double love. He owes his very existence to Lancelot, and he never forgets his father. " Fair lord, salute me to my lord Sir Lancelot my father." The absurd nonsense that has been talked about his being " unhuman and unnatural " misses altogether the matter of the mystically enchanted fatherhood. It loses the significance of that chamber where, as in the Dark Night of the soul, " all the windows and holes were stopped that no manner of day might be seen "; and where the princess of the Grail abandoned her virginity and Lancelot was defrauded of his fidelity, so that the two great Ways might exchange themselves for the begetting of Galahad. The High Prince has remained as an intense symbol of the two Ways; he is not on them, but they are both in him. He is flesh and blood in the union with the Flesh and the Blood.[7]

[7] Professor Vinaver in his *Malory* quotes Mme Lot-Borodine as saying: " *La filiation mystique de Lancelot et de Galaad nous*

In the century or so that followed the august Council there seem to emerge from its shadow and recent presence great moving shapes of organization such as have not been seen before. " In our dealing with the Middle Ages we are often tricked by our imagination. We think of plate armour and of Aristotelianism. But the end of the Middle Ages is already in sight when these attractive things appear."[8] There had been many kinds of groups, of orders, of intellectual and material arrays, before Lateran. But after Lateran they seem to aim more mightily at domination, and if they do not purpose it, yet domination is in their nature, or if even that is too strong, then they are the creatures of a dominant house, a dominant culture, an achieved society. They are everywhere, whether they want to be or not; there is a stability in them as well as in their world, and if, as sometimes happens, one falls, the fall seems to startle and horrify their world. The method of imposition of belief has developed universal organisms; they are seen functioning, each with its particular characteristics. Call them archangelic, and still they are Michael or Gabriel, and no longer the young fledgeling seraphs. And still as they advance, the practice of the Co-inherence seems driven back more and more secretly into the hearts of the saints, who are few in any age.

The world of the thirteenth century may not have had " faith "—in St. Paul's sense. The effort of the Church victorious upon earth had produced a Christendom of a very mixed kind; and not so far beyond the Danube and the Elbe the fighting, metaphysical and actual, was still going on. In 1157 St. Eric IX of Sweden fought the Finns into conversion.

---

paraît certaine, et c'est au sens le plus profond du mot que le premier engendre le second." M. Vinaver points out that this is not borne out " either by the facts of the story or by the principles of the Cistercian doctrine." It seems likely, however, that this is the next movement in the development of the Cycle, since the rest has been done, and Mme Lot-Borodine only wrote in the past tense when she should have written in the future.

[8] *The Allegory of Love,* C. S. Lewis.

A bishopric of Riga was established in 1201; in 1206 the first serious missionary work began to be done in Prussia. Poland had been Christian for centuries, but the Tartar raids interrupted her development and all but destroyed her tradition. The Order of Teutonic Knights fought everyone indiscriminately. But beyond Poland and the Knights, in the district round Kiev and Novgorod and Moscow, the orthodoxy of Byzantium had established itself. It held a perilous world between the Latins in the West and the Tartar "Golden Horde" of Islam in the East. Since the Crusades had eaten Byzantium, however, they were later compelled to disgorge it, the enmity between East and West had grown. In the remote strange plains among all those fighting tribes and peoples the successor to Orthodox Byzantium was being prepared—even while the boundaries of Byzantium itself grew less.

In the West belief—or what passed for belief—was not so pressed. At least Society believed in belief; it believed in the Creed if it did not believe the Creed. It approved, it petitioned for, a new Feast. The doctrine of Lateran was to be made spectacular, and the spectacle was (they said) induced by heaven. Some time after Lateran the inauguration was begun by illumination. "To Juliana, a nun at Mount Cornillon in Belgium, who professed an ardent devotion towards the Body of Christ, a vision came of a full moon whose purity was sullied by one black spot. The moon represented the Church whose liturgical year remained incomplete without the addition of a feast in honour of Christ's Body. Robert, Bishop of Liége, was so impressed that he ordered on his own authority a solemnization of the new festival."[9] In 1264 the new Pope Urban IV, once Archdeacon of Liége, acceded to the request of the faithful, and ordained by the Bull *Transiturus* the celebration of the feast of Corpus Christi everywhere in the Church. The co-inherence of matter and Deity as a presence became as liturgically glorious as it was intellectually splendid, and the performance of the dramatic Mysteries

[9] *Christian-Latin Poetry*, F. J. C. Raby.

and Miracles celebrated in many places through a long summer's day the Act in the present sacrament as well as in history and in the soul. It was organized and exhibited.

As with the processions of Corpus Christi, so with the intrusions (the word means no more than itself) of the Papal complexity of government. It is true that after the Third Innocent, the actual glory at the centre dwindles a little. The declarations are not lessened; nay, they are increased, for in 1302 Boniface, in the Bull *Unam Sanctam* declared formally that the salvation of every human creature depends on his obedience to the Pope. But the persons of the Popes are once more exposed to outrage, as when the soldiers of Philip the Fair of France insult and maltreat the same Boniface in the very next year. The succeeding Pontiff Clement V in some sense modified Boniface's language if not his meaning, and he began the long Papal residence at Avignon among a College composed largely of French cardinals. But whether the claims were stressed or not, and whether the Papal prestige at any moment stood high or low, the Papal organization was more widely spread than ever before. The same Clement took into his own hands and away from cathedral chapters the right of appointing bishops, and in 1344 the right to dispose of all offices and benefices. The grand movement was answered by another; the King of England in 1346 confiscated all benefices held by aliens, and in 1353 the first Præmunire Statute was established. Such things do not directly touch doctrine; they do not deal with definition of boundaries and functions as had the old quarrel about investitures. They are the operation of developed forms; the very quarrel is between accepted stabilities.

The formularized and general activity of the Holy Office is of the same kind; from some points of view it might be regarded as the dark shadow cast, men being what they are, by Corpus Christi. Justifiable or unjustifiable, the jurisdiction of the Inquisition began now as never before to disinherit the bodies of the heretically guilty from every kind of co-inherence. It burned everything outside its own view of co-inherence. Persecution had been formally defined in 1184; in 1215 at Lateran the Council had formally decreed that heretics should suffer confiscation and banishment—and banishment eventually would be, by the nature of things, from all Christendom. In 1252 Innocent IV revived an old pagan habit. He permitted and encouraged the use of torture. Popes and saints and doctors had in the past rejected with horror the very thought. But the reconciliation with time and the manners of fallen humanity had gone deep. The Bull *Ad Extirpanda* decreed—precisely extirpation. The judges of the Inquisition moved from place to place receiving testimony, trying and torturing the accused, effecting judgment, and either releasing under penance or keeping indeterminately in prison, or handing over to the magistrates : " We abandon you to the secular arm, beseeching it affectionately, as Canon Law requires, that the sentence of the civil judges may spare you death or mutilation." In such formulæ the ecclesiastical authorities disguised their intentions. Yet it is to be admitted that the formula itself was a witness to the lasting fact that Canon Law forbade a cleric to be concerned with the shedding of blood. He who served the altars of the One Immolation must not ever be concerned with lesser immolations; the Blood he communicated withdrew him from any other, unless indeed martyrdom should compel him to unite his own with that. The officers who sacrificed the God must not sacrifice men. They did, by a manipulation of words. But the repudiation of such things that was to come centuries later was not without its derivation from the divine Compassion uncompassionately preserved, and perhaps the Single Sacrifice in this also has been with the Church to the end of the world. At that time, for all the individual agonies or local quarrels between inquisitors and princes or inquisitors and bishops, the thing was again a great shape of established power—accepted, habitual, immense.

So also were the new Orders of the thirteenth century, living creatures of yet another kind. Round about 1220 the Pope Honorius III approved and blessed the two great companies of Friars, the Preaching Friars and the Friars Minor, the Dominicans and Franciscans. They too went everywhere; they taught, prayed, lectured, argued, preached. Perhaps in them the alteration between the initiation and the institution is most clearly seen, between the flash and the prolongation. It is not suggested that the children of Francis and Dominic are unworthy of their Founders. But the Orders have a proper stability in time which Francis and Dominic could not have nor could desire to have. They looked to, they hastened to, their end; the Orders cannot do as much.

In the intellectual life similar great forces trampled the earth. The recovery of Aristotle at the end of the twelfth century, at first repudiated and prohibited as a public danger, provided eventually the armour of the grand philosophical minds of the day. Certainly there had been systems of thought before St. Albert and St. Thomas, and certainly St. Thomas himself was not adequately received for fifty years or so after his death; his championship of Aristotle nearly ruined his reputation. But presently Aristotelianism was accepted; it became the panoply of those mammoth systems, for when we contemplate the work of Duns Scotus crashing against that of Aquinas it is of some such conflict of totalitarian minds that we are reminded. Nor has the victory been always to one side; the thought of St. Thomas has been subtly modified by the sensations aroused by Scotus. As, for example, in the effect on our view of matter encouraged by the Scotist opinion that the Incarnation would have happened, had there been no Fall.

" Reason," as Chesterton said, " is always a kind of brute force. . . . The real tyranny was the tyranny of aggressive reason over the cowed and demoralized human spirit." There is, certainly, a way by which Reason can avoid that brutality; it is not a way that St. Thomas took, but it exists. It consists of saying, at the very beginning, as that other great rationalist Euclid said : " Let us suppose. . . ." What we agree to suppose is another matter; it may be that logic can be trusted, or that things exist, or that I can think, or anything else. We cannot begin to prove anything without supposing something. The great Scholastics hardly ever said : " Let us suppose. . . ." Siger of Brabant, who seems to have held that there were two modes of truth, and that one could indeed believe what one knew was not true, may have been trying to get at it. Aquinas defied Siger, but Dante made Aquinas praise Siger. But then poetry can do something that philosophy can not, for poetry is arbitrary and has already turned the formulæ of belief into an operation of faith. We have often been shown how Dante followed Aquinas; it would be of interest to have an exhibition of their differences.[10] For poetry, like faith, can look at the back as well as the front of reason; it can survey reason all round. But the towering castles of the Scholastics would not deign to suppose : it is why the *Inferno* is readable, while the chapters on Hell in the *Summa* are unbearable and unbelievable. Once one has read them, the logical glare of that fire casts a terrible light over the whole *Summa*. But reckless of such feeble humanities the enormous rational disputes went on. The Orders followed their representatives, the Dominicans Thomas, the Franciscans Duns Scotus. There were other teachers. And everywhere the controversies are more sublime, the minds more deeply settled, the teaching more everlasting, the Middle Ages more mightily fixed.

But perhaps the most universal force of all was that of Canon Law. This, which was co-eval with the Church, was first promulgated as a whole by Gregory IX in 1234, nineteen years after Lateran. It received its last medieval addition in 1317, and so remained in force until 1918 in the Roman Church when it was revised, a significant revelation of the two great doctrinal and legislative periods. It was this great body of formulation which controlled and directed most of

[10] Thus for instance, St. Thomas (Part I, Q. 92, Art. 1) says that woman was created as a helper to man " in the work of generation," for in all other works man " can be more efficiently helped by another man." This is hardly the doctrine of the *Comedy*.

men's relationships. It allowed a certain autonomy to secular law, though it retained a right to correct secular law if it erred. It removed, however, to its own jurisdiction all tonsured clerks, though it did not allow this reservation to apply to clerks who had abandoned their calling. It forbade usury. It interfered with war, forbidding it at certain times. It particularly applied itself to the care of widows and injured women. But also it entered into and directed man's most intimate relationships. It controlled the approach to " bed and board." By virtue of its concern with baptism and the new birth it took into its survey all births and all that led to births. The first inviting smile between man and woman brought the two parties under its operative shadow. In that shadow there was established a grand equality between them; it gave little advantage to either. It directed penance for fornication and adultery; it laid down the conditions in which the state called marriage could exist—the state in which " the two parties were themselves the authors of the contract and the ministers of the sacrament. . . . Before the Council of Trent the presence of a priest was not required for the validity of the sacrament."[11] It decreed fasting and feasting; it ordained confession and communion at least once a year; it reserved certain sins to the Pope alone; it declared those matters which excommunicated from the co-inherence on earth. It reached not only to every priest, but to every layman; it professed to declare, not only the necessary organization of salvation, but the very nature of the most intimate organs of men and women.

Sometimes among those powers there was the sound of a terrible overthrow. The thirteenth century had opened with one of the most astonishing of all medieval phenomena —the Children's Crusade. An age like our own of infinite attention to children is defeated by the spectacle; even in the Middle Ages it only happened once. The children pour out from towns and villages, a French boy and a German

[11] *Legacy of the Middle Ages,* G. C. Crump and E. F. Jacob (*Canon Law* : Gabriel le Bras).

boy leading them. They cross the Alps, they descend on Genoa, on Rome; they wait upon miracles. They are to do what Richard Plantagenet could not do; they are to redeem Jerusalem. They excite piety, admiration, greed. The doom closes on them, and they are betrayed. They die of hunger, they are sold as slaves; the capitalists of the day made profit out of them, and it is as if with them some strange quality and capacity of freshness passed from Europe which not all the dogmatic glory of Lateran could revive, nor even the learned subtle piety of the *Pange, lingua* when St. Thomas adored the Sacrament in great verse.

That freshness, however, remained still in one place— in literature, and especially in one convention in literature— the green plot where so much poetry began. *The Romaunt of the Rose, Piers Plowman, Pearl,* to name only three examples, all start with a dreamer and a space of green grass and running water. Beyond that opening into landscape and fresh air they pass to different things, to the garden of courtly love, to the field-fair of the populace, to the other river-bank of heavenly souls. Their sound varies with their concern. But the places of their beginnings are similar, are almost identical, and the song of birds. The song of St. Thomas was immensely valuable to Europe, but it indicated a change; the processions—secular and religious—began to occupy the grass plot. They suited better with the wood of the opening of the *Divine Comedy;* the birds, like the children, easily perished.

A century later a great capitalist institution, which had once had the same purpose as the children, became the centre of the attention of Europe. In 1307 all the Templars in France were arrested by the orders of the King of France. The organisms were turning upon each other; the Inquisition was used against the Templars. It is impossible to know how much of the evidence and confessions can be trusted or not: whether the strange idol, the obscene kisses, the spitting on the Cross, the renunciation of Christ, or the invalid Masses. An English servitor of the Temple, Thomas Tocci de Thoroldeby, deposed that he " for many years past had never seen the Host without thinking of the devil, but that very morning he had heard Mass with great devotion and without any such thought."[12] But in England the examinations do not seem to have been pushed to the extreme; the Pope even suggested that the English Templars should be sent over to France. In France the thing seems to have turned eventually round the rather mysterious figure of the Grand Master Jacques de Molay. " There is an under-current of hostility displayed by the Order itself against Jacques de Molay and against some of the higher officials. . . . Long before the arrest English boys had learned to say 'Beware of the kiss of the Templars.' "[13] What is clear is that, within or without the Order, a kind of darkening of the imagination had taken place. It was easier to think of blasphemy and sacrilege. A kind of luxuriance of diabolic thoughts begins to spread; whether accusers or accused were justified—which we cannot know—it remains true that a certain high corruption of the idea was present. The cats said to be worshipped by witches, by the Templars, by heretics, seem like the wild nightmares of the devout, and so does the human head " very pale and discoloured," " from the neck to the shoulders covered with gold, silver, and precious stones " which was carried by a priest to the altar among processional lights, on the Feast of St. Peter and St. Paul, at the General Chapter of the Order in Paris.[14] The deposition, made in 1308, was, no doubt, false. But someone thought of it, and many liked to think of it. The anxious guard kept against the Devil was doing its ancient work; it was bringing the devil back with power. All through the fifteenth century the speed of his return quickened. The witch-hunts began to open; the *Malleus Maleficarum* was published in 1486; the imposition of belief grew more wild and more ingenious and more cruel. As if in a procession of lights, among fires and screams, the pale and discoloured head—as of a more awful Victim—is carried by the priesthood to the altar.

[12] *The Trial of the Templars*, E. J. Martin.   [13] Ib.   [14] Ib.

CHAPTER VI

CONSUMMATION AND SCHISM

The end of the Middle Ages can be variously regarded as a break-down, a break-up, or a break-through. The last is the least probable; the Middle Ages were not so precluded from intelligence that the discovery of a number of new facts or even of other methods of enjoyment need have much destroyed their balance. They were not, as we now realize, enclosed in narrow dogmas; the dogmas in which they were enclosed were as broad as creation, as high as the top-most movement of the soul, as deep as the genesis of the blood, and as remote as Adam and the Day of Judgment. Such, whether considered macrocosmically or microcosmic-ally, the principles of Christendom must always be; whether they are seen through all times and all places, or in a single human shape. It is true that there were certain things the Middle Ages did not stress, and perhaps the lack of those things contributed to their wreck; as, for instance, they did not habitually encourage the principle of disbelief. The faith of the Middle Ages accepted Reason as implicitly as it accepted Christ; a later age was to be led by the Holy Spirit into the realization that faith can take pleasure in the defeat of rational support while taking advantage from rational support. All this, however, hardly supports sufficiently the image of the Middle Ages " breaking through " into a happier intellectual state. Nor do we normally now believe that they did.

They broke up certainly, into the nations and the classes and the churches. They broke down, through the Black Death and the Great Schism and natural sin. But before the most intense exhibition of that break and means to a break is discussed, something perhaps may be said of two books—

or rather of one book, and one collection of books—in which the imagination of Christendom at that time expressed itself. The first is the *Cloud of Unknowing;* the second is the works of Dante. The Way of the Rejection of Images and the Way of Affirmation of Images had hardly been better expressed before, nor perhaps since. Patmore was almost right when he said of religious poets that there had been

> *from David unto Dante none,*
> *And none since him.*

What there has been since him is a vast number of comments; one additional cannot do much harm.

The effort in Christendom of the polarizing of sex-relationships towards God had been officially disapproved since the Councils of Elvira and Nicaea except in marriage, nor on the whole had much been done to encourage the great experiment even within the limits of marriage. In the general effort of establishing and maintaining a settled civilization marriage had become rather a fixity of social life than a dynamic of divine things. It is extremely doubtful whether monogamy can be defended on the grounds of its being a cultural success; and to do the Church justice she never has tried to defend it primarily on any such unsatisfactory grounds. She has based her defence on the supernatural, and the supernatural and the cultural do not, always and habitually, agree. But for long, affected by her early passion of devotion and her later passion for Reason, she deprecated sexual passion altogether. " The medieval theory finds room for innocent sexuality; what it does not find room for is passion, whether romantic or otherwise. . . . In its Thomist form the theory acquits the carnal desire and the carnal pleasure, and finds the evil in the *ligamentum rationis,* the suspension of intellectual activity."[1]

From this point of view passion towards a man's wife was as bad as passion towards somebody else's wife. The unlimited remark of Messias that a man who desired a woman —nor did he exclude wives—committed adultery with her

[1] *The Allegory of Love,* C. S. Lewis.

was taken literally, and indeed any modification *is* arbitrary. Marriage therefore might easily become an occasion of sin, only redeemable by a strong devotion towards "justice." Justice was, in everything, the pattern-word of the Middle Ages. Marriage was, in its kind, the Justice of the City; the partners had to be "fair" towards each other; they had to exchange permitted, but only natural, satisfactions.

There arose through the centuries—as a parody, as a rival, as a complement, as an inspiration—another idea. "The general impression left on the medieval mind by its official teachers was that all love—at least all such passionate and exalted devotion as a courtly poet thought worthy of the name—was more or less wicked. This impression, combining with the nature of feudal marriage . . . produced in the poets a certain wilfulness, a readiness to emphasize rather than to conceal the antagonism between their amatory and their religious ideals."[2]

This wilfulness underwent changes. But among its results was a tendency to contradict the official tendency towards Reason. The poets said, with Wordsworth, that passion itself was "highest reason"; they did not always add "in a soul sublime." It began to be asserted that "passion" precisely excited and illuminated the intellect, that it delivered from *accidia*, excited to *caritas*, and even (strangest reversal of all!) that such a passion could exist as or in marriage. The idea of marriage as a way of the soul became a possibility. Passion was no longer to be only a morally dubious because un-intellectual quality of marriage, which was itself but a degree of justice working itself out in the world. The discovery of a supernatural justice between two lovers was passion's justification, and yet not only justification, but its very cause. There was vision (or conversion) and there was co-inherence and there was faith and hope and the Christian diagram of universal good-will. In the early days of Christendom, the betrothed couple had been supposed to let the bishop know of their intention. "The Church played the part of the

[2] Ib.

customary *conciliator* or *conciliatrix,* the agent by whom the parties were introduced and commended to each other." This referred primarily to the Rite of marriage; it is still the formal limit of the Rite. But there has been more to it than this. In certain states of romantic love the Holy Spirit has deigned to reveal, as it were, the Christ-hood of two individuals each to other. He is himself the *conciliator* and it is there that the "conciliation"—and the Reconciliation—begins. But this is possible only because of the Incarnation, because "matter is capable of salvation," because the *anthropos* is united with the *theos,* and because the natural and the supernatural are one Christ.

"As many," it was said at the beginning of the Middle Ages, "as are the souls of the faithful, so many are the theophanies."[3] This is a phrase of which the other side is contained in a phrase of Dante's: "the essence is created for the sake of the function and not the function for the essence." The soul, that is, exists to know God, but not God to be known by the soul, and so throughout. The whole work of Dante is an exhibition of a process—the process of the preparation of the essence for its function (the particular essence in question throughout that work, namely, Dante, having been ruined, it is understood, by its co-inherence in whatever is meant by the Fall). It is a process according to the Affirmative Way. It begins when a boy and a girl meet in the streets of Florence; it ends when the whole web of interchanging creation pour themselves towards the *Deivirilis* (to borrow a word from the Areopagite) within the point of Godhead. In this process, which is gradually exhibited in the process of the books, in this point, which is at once the whole content and the whole container of all the books, all the principles of action exist.

The analysis of the early meetings of the boy and the girl is in the *New Life*—a perfectly ordinary boy and girl, except for his single capacity to make great poetry, and except for the fact that there is this particular kind of romantic moment.

[3] *John Scotus Erigema,* Alice Gardner.

The boy, Dante, is very conscious of the three movements aroused in him—the physical, the spiritual, and the intellectual. His brain, as he looks at the girl, tells him in a flash : " Now your beatitude has appeared to you." All the rest of his work contained and examined that fact, however wide its scope. But he did not say : " Beatrice apart from God is your beatitude."

The figure of Love in this book develops along the affirmation of images—of Beatrice, of other women, of Florence, of the Empire, of the Church, of Christ, of events. It is profoundly concerned to communicate virtues such as humility and goodwill, and at last it becomes almost in itself a theophany. But then Beatrice dies. This removal of an image is not at all the same thing as the rejection of images; in fact it does but allow the arrival of a greater image. In the *New Life,* possibly for contemporary reasons, Beatrice had not been shown as active. The *New Life* exhibits the passion of Dante for Beatrice. But the *Comedy* exhibits the passion of Beatrice for Dante.

Between the two are the other books. They are the exposition of principles of art, of ethics, of politics. The activities of body, mind, and spirit are to be concerned not only with the lady but with the City. Dante is a Ghibelline; that is, he attributes as much authority as possible to secular rule, as he attributes as much theophany as possible to individual vision. Neither, however, is allowed to derogate from the business of the official organization of Christendom. He attributes to the clergy their function, and he demands that they shall exist for their function, as the Emperor for his, and he himself for his, and all lovers for theirs. All things exist by each other, and each thrives according only to its fulfilment of its function.

The betrayal of the function by the commanded essence, which is sin, has one chief spectacular example : it is himself. In the *New Life* he had begun the Way. He contemplates the " noble beauty "; he receives, temporarily, communicated virtues; he increases in vision, faith, and power. But Beatrice

—disappears. Two things then seem to happen (i) he contemplates the original beauty in another theophany called
" the Lady at the Window," (ii) he does, at times, ignore and
forget—almost apostatize from—his particular function. He
writes about the " Lady of the Window " almost as if she
were Beatrice. But one can hardly imagine that this is what
Beatrice so passionately denounces in the *Comedy*. He should
have been faithful, she said, to " *mia carne sepulta*," my buried
flesh. But to make this cover the " Lady of the Window "
would be to demand a fidelity from which even the Church
—since its very early days—had blenched. Something of
the irritation of a living woman may have gone into the
indignation of the redeemed Beatrice as something of the
subtlety of a living woman certainly went into Milton's
unfallen Eve. But to make the Repentance of Dante depend
—at that moment—on an unparticularized suggestion of
lechery is hardly convincing; he has abandoned something
greater—what? the Idea itself, perhaps; the very thing for
which he was given those graces and gifts—the Dantean
function of Dante. He has gone *per via non vera,* by a false
way; whereas, at the first sense of change or transition, he
should have followed the first virtue away from such concerns.
The death of Beatrice is the removal of vision; there is
the test of intelligence; there is the work of the quality of
" faith." It is not anything less than itself which should
attract the mind that has known what is greater than all
Nature and all art; and Dante sees, at the moment of her
rebuke, the image of Beatrice turning to the Gryphon who
is " *sola una persona in due nature* "; with such a dramatic
moment of common human experience of sex were the
high dogmas there united. Christ was *anthropos* and *theos*;
so, after its kind, is human and romantic love.

But Dante has turned aside; he has, as in a coma,
wandered. He comes again to himself; he re-finds himself
suddenly—middle-aged, alone, bewildered, in a savage and
obscure wood, wild things terrifying and defeating him,
and beyond them the unapproachable Mountain of his

divined joy. At that moment the world of beatitude, the whole glory of things as they are, aware of his peril rushes to his aid. The Theotokos (individual, but also the universal image of a universal fact) startles Lucy, and Lucy Beatrice, and Beatrice plunges from her place into the resigned peace where those powers dwell who are not Religion though they subserve Religion, and cries to the courtesy of Virgil for help. It is thus the passionate and directed love of Beatrice which begins and sustains the *Comedy*; she of whom we know nothing except that she could be believed to do so, nothing but that she is the great archetype in poetry of all the *shes,* and yet they are themselves and not she, nothing but that there was a girl who was *that* as she walked and chattered and laughed in Florence—the chief of those few girls who out of all the millions have been caught up by holy Luck into the fame of verse and the everlasting glory of spirit. It is so that she laughs and teases and chatters and explains in heaven, only with a greatness about her, the greatness of heavenly fate, and the customs and metaphysics of the redeemed City. It is through her that energy comes, and as by her the *New Life* had once been written and the poetry of Dante had begun, so now in the newer life it is she who moves Virgil and poetry to initiate the Return.

This Return proceeds by three stages. In a sense they may be taken, as they often have been, as the equivalents of the three stages of the formal mystical road. But they are not a record but a poem; they are Dante's vision, not his personal experience (or we do not know that), and they are a great deal beside the Way of Romantic Love. We may observe, however, that each part begins with a single moment of " love," and each moment is related to the equivalent of Beatrice, though they vary. The first is just within Hell; the image is that of Paolo and Francesca, and that moment is so tender and heart-rending in its beauty and horror that Dante cannot bear it. In fact it is most easily credible if it is taken in relation to all that follows. It is the lovers sinking into themselves and refusing everything beyond themselves, and it is this process which is followed up in the descent of the Pit. For from hearing of that thrilling indulgence of a mutual concentration the two visiting spirits inevitably descend to the sight of the indulgence of single and separated concentrations. The greed of love (too exquisite, too lovely, too unselfish, for the word " greed " could the word be avoided) sinks into the greed of gluttony; and then beyond that it develops into the hatred of all who have other and different desires, so that the spendthrifts and the misers butt at each other with great stones. But as the mournful everlastingness of its indulgence and its greed and its hate increases it finds itself in the swamp and the mire of *accidia,* of the state which follows too often after greed and hate; and away in the midst of the black lake are the burning mosques of a more dreadful hell. In that City are the heretics, and what here are the heretics? those who have followed their own mental choice against known authority; therefore those who have petrified their minds into themselves and their desires. The first moment of rash and unrecollected love here, unrepentant and unredeemed, fixes itself on its own fall—at best, like Farinata, it holds its pain in scorn—and what is that but a so second-best? and therefore no best at all —and the circles narrow into darker mysteries, until (after that terrible moment when Dante finds himself *enjoying* hell) the last distance opens across the ice, and everything is reversed, and courtesy itself has to be put off, and far in the midst the traitors to " lords and benefactors," to the City, to the common thing, are champed by what they wished under the monotonously beating wings of the last slavering imbecile, and he is completely *alone.*

But the other moment of love which opens the *Purgatorio?* It is when Casella, Dante's friend, sings Dante's own song back to him, and as the spirits linger to be enthralled by the sound of that lovely, and intellectual, exchange of gifts— a descant on the nature of Love—they are startled by the shout of Cato, the guardian of the ascent; and because it was indeed that kind of song they heard they skirr onwards; they have not intentionally delayed, nor have they meant to forget the laws; now from that lovely interchange of love (so near to the Francescan interchange, differing only perhaps in that the one has intellect and examination, which the other had not) they skirr up the Mountain which is the cause and occasion of all joy, and is found to be the Mount of Repentance and Purgation—that is, of freedom, for the declaration of Christendom is that Repentance is Freedom, not only in the present and future but also in the very past of which the soul repents. Two voices, at least, have said that—Dante himself and the Lady Julian of Norwich (who in many of her thoughts was not so unlike Dante). It is in the tenth Canto of the *Paradiso* that one of the spirits declares that her conscience " gladly allows to her the cause of her lot," her station which is what it is because of her fault; and the Lady Julian says that sin itself is the cause of joy in heaven. But all this is for those who are adult in love, and few, even in Christendom, are those, and fewer those who have left images of that maturity. All up that Mountain the principle of exchange is invoked—intercession, intermediation, the prolongation of that first Casellan moment of substituted song. All the progress is the spiral of this, and all the maxims. It is at the end that the great recognition of the transmuted first love takes place: " look well; we are, we are indeed Beatrice."

" Look well " is the maxim of the Paradises, which also open with a moment of love. Here the spirit Piccarda in the lowest heaven is asked if she does not begrudge others their greater beatitude, and she answers that love contents all wills, that there love is *necesse*, is fate, that in fact if you love anyone you do not envy them—the whole question is nonsense. And it is seen to be nonsense in phrase after phrase: perhaps the greatest from this point of view is the high intensity of celestial interchange when Dante cries to Folco of Marseilles in the third heaven, of Venus: " did I in-thee myself as thou dost in-me thyself." The recurrent image of this in-meing and in-theeing is the eyes of the Florentine girl, which had reflected the two-natured Gryphon—and all the Paradises are the anatomy of the Gryphon—and now laugh at the man she loves so that his mind is at one point drawn away from the union with God (for which he is not yet ready) and splintered into an awareness of the great intellectual doctors of the Church who then surround him. This is an example of the Way of Affirmation; it is the substantial body of Beatrice which is the measure and the link of all that know-ledge—" *la carne gloriosa e santa,*" and again, " the organs of the body shall be strong for all that means delight." And when Beatrice leaves Dante's side, St. Bernard who takes her place has no other doctrine; without the body the soul cannot be consummated in God. It is these great doctrines of matter, of exchange, of perfect love, which are made apparent in the paradox of the line "*Vergine Madre, figlia del tuo Figlio.*" This is the secret of the universe, the mortal maternity of Godhead; beyond is but the ray of Godhead which contains all. Dante gazes still; " look intently; look." But it was the face of the girl in Florence which first startled him into looking.

It is not without some relevance to the history of Christen-dom to notice that when the little book which recounted that original start, when the *New Life,* was at last printed —in 1576—the ecclesiastical authorities censored it. There had been some difficulty over Dante altogether; which is not surprising so far as the political *De Monarchia* is con-cerned. That had been taken up by some of the Reformers, and one edition (it is said) had even been seen through the press by Foxe of the Protestant martyrology. But the *New Life* was not noticeably Calvinistic, nor do the eyes of Beatrice in the *Comedy* flash with Lutheran, though they do with reforming, fire. No; but the language of the *New Life* was extreme and dangerous. The officials got to work on it. They cut all references to Beatrice as " *beatitudo* " and sub-stituted " *felicita* "; they cut " *salute* " and substituted " *quiete* " or " *dolcezza* "; they cut the " *Osanna* " with which the angels received the soul of Beatrice; they cut the profound allusion to the girl Giovanna going before Beatrice, as John the Baptist went before the True Light. In short, they took immense care to alter the whole point of Beatrice; they laboured to explain that this was merely an ordinary love-affair, and that no love-affair could be more than an unilluminated love-affair. In a positive terror of the flesh they abolished everything but the flesh. It was their bad luck, though by 1576 they might have known they were dealing with Dante, and by 1576 they might have known that most lovers feel as Dante felt. It is one of the drawbacks of a celibate priesthood that they are bound to the personal rejection of that particular image.

They had, it must be admitted, their own doctors against the work of Dante; against the *Comedy*, the *Cloud of Unknowing* aspires translucently, and no colours of earth shade it. It is supposed to have been written in the middle of the fourteenth century, some score of years after Dante died. The author of it (so its last editor suggests) was a " master " of Oxford or Cambridge who became the rector of some country parish, and there lived that life of contemplation to which his books testify.[4] He is unknown; nothing could be more right. His book was not written merely for readers; indeed it is all but impossible to read it. For it begins :

In the name of the Father, and of the Son, and of the Holy Ghost.

I charge thee and I beseech thee, with as much power and virtue as the bond of charity is sufficient to suffer, whatsoever thou be that this book shalt have in possession, whether by property, or by keeping, or by bearing as a messenger, or else by borrowing, that inasmuch as in thee is by will and advisement, thou neither read it, write it, nor speak it, nor yet suffer it to be read, written, or spoken, by any other or to any other, unless it be by such a one or to such a one as hath (in thy supposing) in a true will and by a whole intent purposed him to be a

[4] *The Cloud of Unknowing,* Dom Justin McCann.

perfect follower of Christ. And that not only in active living, but also in the sovereignest point of contemplative living the which is possible by grace to be come to in this present life by a perfect soul yet abiding in this deadly body.

Dante had written for, as it were, all the world, and all the world has neglected seriously to study him. The Oxford master (or whoever) protested against the world, and the world is aware of him. He is a text, an example, a type. It has been said of him : " That the name and reputation of this successful spiritual guide—undoubtedly one of the most interesting personalities in the long line of English mystics —should have faded into complete obscurity is one of the minor tragedies of history." He was " one of the most interesting personalities " when he wrote : " not what thou art, nor what thou hast been, doth God regard with his merciful eyes, but what thou wouldst be." And that a man may never " by the work of his understanding come to the knowing of an unmade ghostly thing : the which is nought but God. But by the failing he may. Because that thing that he faileth in is nothing else but only God." He was— God in heaven!—" a man of strong individuality "; he was " a lovable man." It is " a tragedy " that he has " faded into complete obscurity "—he who wrote his whole book for nothing but that, who forbade anyone to touch it unless he desired that, who made that his title, his prologue, and his ending. " Travail busily," he said, " in that nought." In a very different sense we do precisely so.

It is, in fact, as that divine student knew, of the essence of the Negative Way that only such students can properly write of it. It may be added that probably the same thing is true of the Affirmative, or Dante and Beatrice would not have become the sentimentalized hackneys of our ancient idealistic cab. But at least the images of the Way of Affirmation correspond to something, whereas not sanctity, not piety, but the mere decency of human courtesy removes the other path from any such book as this present. The charge and challenge of that

most blessedly unknown cartographer of heaven cannot easily
be overcome. It must be sufficient to note that he set himself
against—not so much the body as—"a proud, curious, and
imaginative wit." He held indeed, like so many Christian
saints, that the body was of high use and companionship to
the soul, and that God would "reward man his meed in bliss
both in body and soul." But the forsaking of the world,
the "cloud of forgetting," the finding of humility (which is
but to know things as they are), the refusal "in the time of
this work" to know any familiar or private affection, for in
that working "shall all be equally dear to him; for he shall
feel then no other cause but only God"—all this and much
else is the contradiction of "the proud curious wit" such
as, it was said, had in the beginning received the fair gracious
co-inherence of all mankind and had as a result raised up
enmity and division and perverse desire. The two ways are
described in the book itself, with the emphasis on its own:

Yea—and if it be courteously and seemly to say—
in this work it profiteth little or nought to think of the
kindness or the worthiness of God, nor on our Lady,
nor on the saints or angels in heaven, nor yet on the joys
of heaven; that is to say, with a special beholding to them,
as though thou wouldst by that beholding feed and in-
crease thy purpose. . . . For although it be good to think
upon the kindness of God, and to love him and praise him
for it; yet it is far better to think upon the naked being
of him, and to love him and praise him for himself.

Yes? yes. Yet even that blessed creature could not define
all the ways. It was on the very verge of utmost blessedness,
at the consummation of the motion through which she had
brought him, exercising a million images on their way, that
Dante flung out the great opposite cry to the Florentine
girl: "O lady, in whom my hope lives, and who hast set
thy feet in hell for my safety, in all the things I have seen
I recognize the grace and virtue of thy worth and of thy goodness; thou hast brought me from slavery to freedom along
every path and in every manner of which thou hadst the

power; guard thine own magnificence in me, so that my
spirit, which thou hast healed, may be pleasing to thee when
it leaves the body!" And in the very last canto, a hundred
lines from the end, all the images appear at Bernard's call:
" See," he cries to the Mother of the Son, " see where Beatrice
with how many of the blest entreat thee with clasped hands."
The eyes of the Theotokos smile back; it is the last and
greatest image, but an image it is.

There were many others of that age—in that century and
the next, as in all—who pursued the End. There were others,
such as the well-meaning Marjory Kempe, who seems to
have been stirred by a real convulsion of the soul, but who
was certainly an example of the difficulty the officials of the
Church had in controlling the wilder enthusiasms. She lived
in that same century, and she had " married beneath her."
Before her conversion she was difficult with her husband
owing to her worldly rank; afterwards she was still more
difficult owing to her heavenly vocation. She wanted them
both to live chaste, and would have nothing to do with him
maritally, thus ruining the very " justice " of marriage. She
had a way of bursting at any moment into tears and sobs,
interrupting sermons or whatever, and rather taking the
confusion she created as a work of the Holy Spirit. She
also had communication with our Lord, who encouraged her
by expressing severe displeasure with anyone she thought
hostile. It had not been his habit on earth with the sons
of thunder. She paid a call on the Lady Julian at Norwich,
to whom apparently she told a long tale of God's grace to her:
" compunction, contrition, sweetness and devotion, compassion
with holy meditation and high contemplation, and full
many holy speeches and dalliance that Our Lord spake to
her soul; and many wonderful revelations, which she showed
to the anchoress to find out if there were any deceit in them,
for the anchoress was expert in such things, and good counsel
could give."[5]

The Lady Julian listened and praised God. But she also

[5] *The Book of Marjory Kempe,* edited by W. Butler-Bowdon.

delivered a short monologue on the nature of charity, and it seems likely that she was more expert than Marjory Kempe quite understood. " The Holy Ghost moveth ne'er a thing against charity, for if He did He would be contrary to His own self, for He is all charity." She encouraged Marjory, however, to have patience, and sent her happily on her way—to rebuke bishops, to be a general nuisance, but to be always, perhaps foolishly but certainly sincerely, concerned with her Lord.

This, however, was after 1400, and by then other and wider convulsions had taken place. Dante had died in 1321. The century was not ended before two great blows fell respectively on the body and the mind of Western Christendom and by the end of the century the last fortress of Eastern Christendom was all but lost. The two blows were the Black Death and the Great Schism. The vast poetic consummation of medieval (the word is perhaps desirable) Christendom had gone almost beyond itself in an effort to present the perfect union, and indeed it was immediately read and studied. The great mystics of that century were speaking or keeping silence in their separate places. But as if the consummation was to be prevented, the body and intelligence of Christendom were twice attacked, and though Christendom recovered, it recovered to find itself beginning to live a different kind of life from that to which it had been, for some three centuries, accustomed.

The Black Death appeared first in the Crimea in 1346, in Sicily in 1347, at Venice and Genoa in January 1348. It had passed through Europe and was at the edge of the Narrow Seas by the end of June; in the beginning of July it appeared in England. In that six months it had slain, it would seem, wherever it touched, as many as or perhaps more than it left alive. Cities were desolated; great buildings were left for ever unfinished; monasteries and chapters were reduced to a few or in some instances to one survivor. The fabric of the Middle Ages endured, for those two or three years, a quaking of the earth. Not only labourers but lords were swept away; not only lord but labourers. The depopulation which struck the mass has been again one of those things from which we have hardly recovered. It was the beginning, in England, and to some extent elsewhere, of those social troubles which were soon to be exacerbated by the wealth of the Renascence. The Middle Ages had authoritatively declared that social justice was a necessary thing, it was accepted as " a terrestrial and carnal projection of the Communion of Saints."[6] It is true that this was too often regarded more as a matter of *caritas* than of *justitia*. But it was *caritas* rather than *justitia* which the Church supposed herself to be primarily encouraging: *justitia* was but the measurement of something that had not achieved *caritas*. It had to be there; it was the extension of *caritas* into the lesser dimensions. It was preached much more than it was followed. But the corruption of the Death struck at more than individuals, and the Middle Ages faltered under it.

But if the Death shook the medieval fabric from below, a thing as bad and perhaps worse broke on it like a storm from above. It is to be remembered that all this time Christendom in the East was becoming more and more hemmed in by the military operations of Islam, and that, whatever Christendom might be, Islam was still very much Islam. Neither Islam nor Christendom ever regarded each other as anything else than a false idea of God. There were, of course, all kinds of treaties, of friendships, of admirations; there were communications and influences. But the undoubted historic fact that it was the Papacy which, in the West, was always crying for a Crusade was due to that philosophical distinction. All through the fourteenth century the line of the Byzantine Empire was pressed further back, and its only permanent ally in the West, with whatever doctrinal reservations, was the Pope.

For some seventy years since 1305 the Popes had been living not in Rome but in Avignon, very much under the direction of the Kings of France. In 1376 Saint Catherine of Siena persuaded or compelled Gregory XI to return to Rome,

[6] *The Poor and Ourselves,* Daniel-Rops.

where he died. The Cardinals proceeded to Conclave, on 7 April, 1378, and on 18 April, Easter Sunday, the new Pope, Urban VI, was crowned; all the Cardinals were present. It was nearly sixty years since the death of Dante, and thirty since the coming of the Black Death. The projects of Europe, public and private, proceeded in their normal way. The great accepted institutions functioned. Certainly it was known that in May the Cardinals had left Rome for Anagni, on account of the heat, and it was reported that the new Pope had displayed a new temper, quite different from that he had shown before the election. " Rarely," it was said afterwards, " do the habits of the lords elected change for the better." St. Catherine did what she could : " Holy Father," she begged, " moderate yourself; check your temper."[7] In August the Cardinals suddenly informed all Europe, the Kings and the Universities, that the people of Rome had compelled the Election, that it was invalid, and that there was an Apostate in the See of Peter. On 18 September the Apostate replied by creating practically a new College of twenty-eight Cardinals. The original Cardinals moved to Fondi and there solemnly elected a new Pope, who took the name of Clement VII. They communicated this fact also to the various civil and ecclesiastical Powers. It was a blow, but it had happened before when discontented Cardinals went wandering. Much depended on what happened next. Urban VI took refuge in St. Angelo and tortured half a dozen of his unfortunate new creatures. Clement VII moved about Italy and eventually took ship for France and Avignon. But before he did so, the great University of Paris had made a decision. They had examined, so far as they could, the facts; they recognized the Pontificate of the Lord Clement. The King of France acceded to their decision and in the person of Clement welcomed the true Pope. " He changed the Schism from an event into a movement."

Such breaches had occurred before. This was, as they had

[7] *Inner History of the Great Schism*, G. J. Jordan, from which the quotations are taken.

been, a breach between two sets of facts and not between two sets of dogmas. Both before and after this Schism there were to be pious and holy souls who rejected the claims of the Roman See. But now no one was rejecting any such claims, except, as one might say, the Roman See itself. It was engaged both in promulgating and rejecting its own Pontiff. And the proper identity of that Pontiff was a matter of some considerable importance to Christendom—not as much certainly as it was to be after Constance or Trent or Vatican, but still of urgent importance. The difficulty, as it were, of deciding who was what was enhanced by the fact that the only witnesses to the problem contradicted themselves flatly. If what the Cardinals said in April were true, then what they said in September was not true; if what they said in September, then they had been inaccurate in April. It was left to the Universities, to the Kings, to the Bishops and Dukes, to chapters and councils, in fact to everyone, to decide. There was the Vicar of Christ and his Ape. But which was the Ape?

France had gone with Clement; Italy with Urban. The Empire went with Urban; so did England. Scotland went with Clement. But in each country minorities existed, and minorities within those minorities. Tumults and riots broke out. Property was destroyed and minor crusades initiated, till in 1381 the University of Paris made a move. The Schism had lasted three years, which was wholly unexpected. The obvious way of healing it was by a General Council, extreme step though that might be. But difficulties immediately arose. Only the Pope could call a General Council; and only the Pope could ratify the decisions of a General Council. The duplicated Headship would not coalesce to call a General Council, and any single gathering would leave the other Obedience where it was—unless there should be two General Councils, a thing incredible. The University got as far as to hold a disputation on whether it would be heretical to declare that neither Claimant was Pope. But Canon Law was too much for it; the situation relapsed and went from bad to worse till 1394.

In that year feeling in France was so high that the University sity proceeded to consider other means. The Schism had lasted now for sixteen years, and Western Christendom was no nearer peace at its centre. It was formally proposed that the Way of Cession be adopted; that is, that both Claimants should be persuaded to renounce their holdings. Neither showed any likelihood of doing so. In 1395 a National Council of France sent ambassadors to Avignon, and in 1396 the Imperial Diet, attended by the King of England, sent ambassadors to Rome. A Benedict had succeeded Clement and a Boniface had succeeded Urban. But the new persons clung to Dante's maxim though it was unquoted. All good is dangerous, and so was that. They said they were there to serve their functions. Ambassadors and Cardinals on their knees implored the Pontiffs to concede. They refused; they insisted on functioning.

In 1398 the French authorities were growing desperate. Another National Council proposed a still more drastic step—the Withdrawal of Obedience. The more militant Withdrawers sent an army against Benedict in Avignon and besieged him there. But this action shocked the more moderate party; Benedict, after all, on their view was the true Pope. It was one thing to beg for Cession and another to revolt in war. The University of Toulouse wrote to the King of France, protesting against Withdrawal. Their view was that it had made everything even worse and encouraged all kinds of disorder. When Benedict heard of this he slipped away from Avignon and sent Cardinals to negotiate with the King. The King gave way. The other side had done nothing to enforce Withdrawal on Boniface, and France was tired of being under irresponsible ecclesiastical government. Restitution of Obedience was determined, and carried out in 1403, with appropriate tears and *Te Deums,* the Lord Benedict having first been put on his good behaviour by a treaty. It was in France understood that the Pope, and proclaimed that everyone else, had repented.

The repentance was but moderate. Within three years,

the Schism continuing and Benedict displaying anything but a spirit of peace and reconciliation towards the Church in France, the French authorities took a new line. By 1404 tempers were rising and in 1406 there was a Solemn Disputation, in the course of which the Way of a General Council was again mooted. It was asserted and known to be uncanonical. But reply was made that it was not always a necessity to keep the order of law, for while law was kept, Christians were perishing; "the Pope can err and can sin, but the Church is so full of love that it cannot wander nor err nor commit sin." The aim was to be "Cession by force," and the means were to be Withdrawal of Temporalities. The Church in France pronounced the word "Necessity."

In England the effect of the Schism had been twofold. A Parliament held at Oxford had originally determined to support the King in following the Obedience of Urban. But that did not end the violence of the quarrels, as is seen in the case of John Wycliffe. He at the beginning had approved of Urban. But his chaotically academic mind, his sincere piety, and his violent vocabulary all led him into extremes. He came nearer and nearer to denouncing the Papal theory, and presently he was doing so. He felt—perhaps he exaggeratedly felt—the harm of the Schism; he talked about the Italian as others of the English in our day have talked about another Italian. "The Pope," he said, was "the head vicar of the fiend," "a member of Lucifer." It became more and more clear to him that the Pope was not in a state of grace, and that a state of grace was a condition of all lordship, dominion, and property. Lordship and dominion belong only to those in a state of grace. And who is in grace? Those who follow righteousness and the will of God. And who . . .? alas, the old danger follows—"those who do what I think they ought to do." Dominion and the right to obedience were to depend on character. It is to be admitted that the character of Urban seems to excuse, if any could, the refusal of obedience. Yet if obedience is to depend on character— it was but a variation on the old Gnostic theme: there is a superior set of people in the Kingdom of God. It looks as if Wycliffe thought there were.

Greater authorities would not have it. In London and later at Constance it was decreed that whoever preached that a bishop or priest, being in mortal sin, cannot ordain or baptize, " let him be anathema." The great Gerson declared that those were anathema who laid it down that all *dominium* and *dignitas* were founded *in justitia caritatis*. The Church could not bring itself to assert that a lack of *caritas* in the lord freed his subordinates from obedience. At the same time it was clear that a lack of *caritas* in the Two Claimants was highly embarrassing to the Church, and that an effort was being made to force upon them the Cession that should have been due to *caritas*. What was the justification? any principle? necessity? In effect, necessity : " *pia quaedam necessitas.*"

What followed is one of the most curious episodes in the history of the Western Church. Extreme individualists, like Wycliffe who announced that God had mercifully cloven the head of Antichrist, in order that the two parts might destroy each other, remained practically negligible, except in as far as they expressed in that day the continuous subterranean evangelical Revolt. The *communis sensus* of Christendom rejected them. On the other hand the same " common sense " began at last to have its effect on the Claimants. They were reluctantly forced towards each other. Boniface at Rome had been succeeded by Gregory XII, and both he and Benedict were committed by oaths to cede, if the other did, or if the other died. It was agreed that the Two should meet at Savona. Circling nearer and nearer, they approached, but they never met. A secret communion of reluctance prolonged discussion; date after date was fixed, and date after date went by. " One is a land animal that fears the sea, one a sea animal that fears the land," it was said. Gregory tried to create Cardinals; Benedict to excommunicate afresh all who opposed him. England and France both denounced the "Concurrents." The Cardinals deserted their respective Heads, and sent representatives to Leghorn. By the authority of the Cardinals and the Kings a Council was called at Pisa. Could it be done? No; except "*in casu tam necessario.*" Could the Colleges unite (since one, by definition, must be schismatic)? Necessity. Could obedience be rightfully rendered them? Necessity. Could the Council elect a new Pope? Necessity. And so on. The whole of Christendom was (except for one of the Two Concurrents) *ultra vires*. But the whole of Christendom meant action. The Emperor Rudolf presented twenty-three objections, but the Council desperately overruled them. On grounds of schism, perjury, and suspicion of heresy, it deposed both the Concurrents, and elected another, Alexander V. The Concurrents refused to submit, and each called a Council of his own, though their supporters dwindled daily. Of the three " it was the third Pope, the one of the three who was most certainly not Pope, whom practically the whole of Christendom obeyed."[8] Unfortunately in less than a year Alexander died, and the harassed Council elected John XXIII, an unfortunate of debased character and feeble statesmanship. The Emperor Sigismund at last compelled him to do what he was there to do—convoke a Council. It was, by Canon Law, no more legitimate than Pisa. But it met at Constance, and Necessity (under the shape of the Emperor) controlled it. It burnt John Huss who was full of similar anarchical ideas to Wycliffe. It deposed John XXIII on the usual superb medieval string of charges. And at last, over-awed or repentant or weary, Gregory XII sent letters to the Emperor convoking a Council at Constance and then abdicating. He was eighty-nine, and by that act of an old man's surrender he saved the Papacy (as men say about such things). The Council deposed Benedict, who had fled to Spain and stayed there cursing both the Cardinals and the kings; it proceeded to a new election, and the Lord Cardinal Odo Colonna became Martin V.

Necessity had done its work. It was promptly denied. The Conciliar effort to control the Papacy continued for some twenty years, and failed. The Popes re-established the auto-

[8] *A Popular History of the Church,* Fr. Philip Hughes.

cratic government of Rome as of divine providence. The Council of Pisa was denied to be a Council; the Council of Constance was admitted only from the letters of Gregory. But it remains true that the new Papal success was precisely due to contra-Papal action.

A man who, at the age of 12, had entered the University of Paris and heard the first news of the Second Election in 1378, would have been forty-eight when the Council met at Constance. But a man born in 1378 would have been thirty-six. A whole generation had grown up to manhood and to theological thought in the presence of the Schism, the Two Concurrents, the efforts of the National meetings and of the Kings. He had been used to denunciations and excommunications; he had been used to regarding half-Christendom (his own or the other) as out of regular communion, and in a state of revolt. He had been used to Withdrawals and Restorations of Obedience. He had been used to hearing from, say, Paris or Oxford, that he was to do this or the other ecclesiastically. He had been used to arguments and sermons on the Nature of the Church, of the Hierarchy, of the Papacy. Belief admitted its principles, but their visuality wavered; reason had to find a way round itself. Necessity triumphed; it was denied, but it could not be forgotten. Since its beginnings the Western Church had known no such contradiction—not of theory—but of practice. An ambiguity of apparent fact troubled the whole organization; actuality and reflection were confused. It is inconceivable that the generation—and much more than a generation—which received the shock and the continuity of disunion should not have eased men's minds towards dispute and hostility. The split of the Reformation was already prepared.

Byzantium fell; there opened in all the West the new wealth of the Renascence.

CHAPTER VII

THE RENEWAL OF CONTRITION

In that new and grand outbreak of wealth and diverted energy, it can be seen that the effort to impose upon the half-converted masses the great complex of exchange rooted in redemption had failed. The effort had been made by means of the continual effort towards conversion, through generation after generation, and by the imposition of authoritative command. From the Pope to the acolyte, from the king to the serf, from the scholastic doctor to the least actor in the Mysteries, the effort of converting disobedience through obedience to a love of Reconciliation in obedience had failed, and the effort of compelling obedience by the force of the mere organized means of Reconciliation had failed. It was not, of course, surprising; it was what had always been foreseen. Christendom had betrayed itself again, as, since St. Peter, it was always doing. There was to be, as there always has been, a sharp and violent recall. It was not for nothing that Messias had uttered one of his most appalling and ambiguous sayings : " Behold, I am with you always."

The particular state of things which we call medieval drew to its end in an outbreak of energy, and sometimes a rather feverish energy. The Middle Ages did not know that they were ending but they did know that they were changing. They knew that the East had fallen and that the Turk, that Islam and its Unincarnate Deity, were in Constantinople, and threatening the West. They knew also that Antiquity had returned—in manuscripts, in statues, in prestige. They knew that navigation was expanding. They knew, in fact, that their own Victorian age was past and that a whole new mode of living was at their disposal; they were the heirs of everything. Over all Europe went up a kind of scream of colour. The Middle Ages had had both screams and colour; they had had enough worldliness. But formally they had always, at a certain point, intended to dissociate themselves from worldliness. The admiration there paid to the glory of Man, of *Homo,* had been checked by an awareness of the need of the New Birth. The Renascence tended to forget the need for any other Birth but its own.

The traditional figure of the Renascence used to be Alexander VI. It is impossible not a little to regret the rehabilitation of the Borgias. To remember that the family produced saints is one thing; to make their other members nothing more than respectable worldly princes is quite another. The magnificent and magical figure of Alexander had once, for those who could accept it, a particular attraction. And only morons were repelled by it from the theory of the Papacy. Romantics who were not morons were drawn to it precisely because of the theory of the Papacy. Wicked bishops and wicked kings were common enough. But that the concentration of wickedness—avarice, pride, murder, incest—should exist in the See; that the infallible Vicar should possess the venom and be in love with his own uncanonical daughter; that that daughter should be throned in the Chair itself over adoring Cardinals, and that the younger of her two brothers should assassinate the elder, and the awful three—the Pontiff and the two children—should wind the world into their own skein of lust and cunning . . . this was the kind of thing that demanded the implicit presence of the whole future Roman development. The incarnation of Antichrist (romantically speaking) must be in the See of Christ. The Scandal of the Church had to be a scandal of the True Church, or it lost half its lurid glory.

It seems it was not so. Lucrezia was less lovely and more moral than had been supposed, and Cæsar, if as brilliant, was almost always excusable, and Alexander himself is no more than a great Renascence statesman, and it was most unlikely that he poisoned cardinals or even died of the venom himself; alas, only Christian rites took place in the Pontifical chapels, even if the tapestries were a little pagan. The myth, however, had this to be said for it—it was contemporary. It was no more a late Protestant invention than the other legend of the Lady Joanna, Pontifex Maxima in the Dark Ages. It was accepted by pious and credulous chroniclers of the day. It was the kind of fable the Renascence liked, and it was enjoyed as a myth of that new discovery of the Renascence—*Homo,* Man.

It can hardly be said that the Middle Ages had neglected Man. But then everything that the Renascence carried on was begun in the Middle Ages—science, art, scholarship, exploration. The Middle Ages paid their normal attention to the ordinary affairs of men, as all normal attention must be paid, *semper, ubique, ab omnibus.* When, however, they thought about those affairs, they imagined them in terms of God and grace. And eventually their energy could not live up to the dazzling circle of dogma within which it operated. God was everywhere the circumstance of all lives. Men had been over-nourished on such metaphysics, and the Renascence abandoned the idea of that universal Circumstance to attend to lesser circumstances. Change, sin, and intelligent delight in the creation had all been at work, and now they did not so much break bounds as withdraw from the bounds. The thought of the Middle Ages was not limited, but perhaps its philosophical vocabulary was. Persistently and universally the stress changed. The Lord Alexander VI was no worse than some of the medieval Popes but he was—ever so little —different. He and Julius II and Leo X all accepted the Mass. But it is difficult to think of any of them as being primarily and profoundly concerned with the Mass. They were probably —even Julius—more humane than Urban VI but they were also more human. Urban was said to have read in his Breviary while he listened to the moans and shrieks of the tortured Cardinals; it would have been more characteristic of Alexander to have read pasquinades or love-songs while he caused to be poisoned—if he had done—his prisoner the Lord Giambattista Orsini, Cardinal-Deacon of Santa Maria Nuova.

Erasmus was as Christian as—and much less anti-Papal (so to call it) than—Dante. But the monks, the heavy and certainly stupid monks, who denounced Erasmus were, in a sense, right. There was a great deal to be said for their point of view, though (as so often happens) they themselves were precisely the wrong people to say it. Erasmus can be studied and admired as a devout scholar. He can hardly be ranked as a scholarly devotee. Leonardo was probably a pious, if sceptical, scientist. But he could hardly be said, except in a highly mathematical manner, to exalt piety by science. The opponents of either were no more pious or devout than scholarly or scientific. The habitual and rather worn religious intelligence of the time was not so high that it could afford to abuse Leonardo or Erasmus, as those periods might have done, with a better chance, to which grace was still a dreadful reality. " It is painful," wrote a later bishop[1], " to sit and see and hear men arguing on the exigencies of the human race, and plainly ignorant of all that is passing in the head and heart, of that human race, beyond their own little fragment of it." Meanwhile Machiavelli was writing about men. " We owe thanks," said Francis Bacon later, " to Machiavelli and to writers of his kind who openly and without dissimulation show what men are and not what they ought to be." Certainly Chaucer and Boccaccio had done much the same, but they had remembered what men ought to be. Machiavelli was a one-sided Augustinian; he laid open the secrets of man's natural corruption. It did not prevent his own large-minded honesty from being a simple Christian; it did allow him himself to be regarded as a myth of diabolical wickedness— only so far excusable that it was *Homo* and not *Homo-in-Deo* on which his eyes were observantly turned.

What, to such great men, was the vision of the glory of Man in his capacious intellect, was in lesser men the vision of temporal and decorative glory, and in still lesser the vision of nothing much more than gold. Gold still for delight, for

[1] Bishop Ullathorne, 2 July, 1870. *The Vatican Council*, Dom Cuthbert Butler.

ornament, for display, as well as for possession, but still gold.
The Middle Ages had desired greatness and glory and gold as
much as their children; virtue after them was not so very much
impaired. But the metaphysical vision which had illuminated
those otherwise base things was passing; they were no longer
mythological beyond themselves. Man was left to take glory
in, and to glorify, himself and his works. Had chances been
different, there might then have been a revival of the old
wisdom of Christ as *anthropos*; the secrets of Christendom
might have enriched with new significance the material world.
It was not to be; the *anthropos* had been forgotten for the
theos, and now the other *anthropos*, the Adam of Augustine,
the *homo sapiens* of science, preoccupied European attention.

But the *Homo* was, at points, compacted and solidified. The
Prince arose, and the separate Princes. The rise of the nations
had exalted those figures of surrounding kingship to more
and more of a formal equality with their centre the Emperor.
The Empire had been lost to Islam in the East; it was lost to
Europe in the West. It was to linger there uncertainly till
1805, as in the East it was to be half-revived in Muscovy
until 1917. The Great Schism had encouraged the Thrones,
for the decision between Pontiff and pseudo-Pontiff—the
decision which of them was which, the decision which of them
was canonically and righteously which, and where grace
lay—had depended largely on the Thrones. A hundred
years had nearly passed, but the vibration lingered as the
vibration of Napoleon lingers to-day. It lasted the longer
because, by a natural impulse, the Throne of Peter became
one also among the Thrones. The Lord Alexander VI claimed,
formally, to be sovereign over sovereigns; but his alliances
and his armies and his treaties compelled him to be regarded
as a Prince by the Princes. " The Lord Alexander VI was a
very great man "[2]—so; but his manhood preoccupied the
world more than his Vicariate, and by an inevitable process
both he and his allies and his opponents tended to regard
Christ—in his Church—as the Vicar of the Roman See rather

[2] *The House of Borgia,* F. Rolfe (called Baron Corvo).

than the Roman See as the Vicar of Christ. Messias was a province of the hierarchy and of the Head of the hierarchy. It was but a part of the general change. Louis XI was even more superstitious than Louis IX but he was less supernatural. The Emperor Maximilian had some thoughts of making himself Pontiff, thoughts which would hardly have occurred to St. Louis. The sacerdotal was a rank in the aristocracy, but the saintly had lost its appeal. It had ceased to be fashionable, and even when only fashionable sanctity has about it an energy in which the very fashions tremble. But now for awhile it was not much more than one of its own relics.

Homo, that is, had entered religion also. The cry of " Another is in me " had faded, and the Renascence glory was not attributed to the Acts of that Other. Christ was encouraged, at need, to act the deeds of *Homo*; hardly his own. At this particular moment in the history of Christendom acts had got largely out of hand. Faith (in St. Paul's sense) was, no doubt, much practised secretly but the most characteristic spectacular acts lacked its validity. The acts of a man without that validity tend to involve his lower nature more and more, and even the imaginative acts of the Renascence did not reach to " the top of speculation," except perhaps in the effort of Leonardo to measure the very angle of creation itself. The *Mona Lisa* is the effort of art to discover and pattern the very first creative movement of a smile; the whole superb labour of its painter discovered in creation the mathematical motion towards a similar ostentation. And even the vision of heart's peace so dear to Erasmus may have demanded for its full affirmation a second series of acts for which perhaps the great scholar knew his own incapacity.

The cry for Reform which is always heard in the Church was no less vocal then. It had always been admitted that a certain magnificence was becoming to the secular ritual of the Church. Ritual and magnificence were now becoming vices, and the austerer minds felt them so; nor was there discoverable, as so often there had been, a compensating energy in the convents and hermitages. Convents had become the subject of anxious consultation everywhere, which is not to say that they deserved it everywhere. But Another was no longer lucidly within their inhabitants; the lives which those inhabitants did not noticeably lay down for their brethren, as Clement of Alexandria had taught, attracted the attention of both better and worse men. The reforming party clamoured, as always, for alteration, and were, as always, right. But because they were always clamouring and always right, no effective action was taken. They declaimed like the Communist leaders of our own day. They directed their attacks pointedly to the personal lives of the ecclesiastical officers. It is only of recent years that that personal attack has seemed to fail. Few Roman Catholics now denounce the secret vices of the Pope; few Anglicans exhibit the loathsome corruption of their Archbishops; no President of any Free Church Council is accused of sodomy or sloth. Perhaps indeed their lives are more pure, or perhaps vociferousness has merely exhausted itself.

Nevertheless a crisis approached, and the sublime discretion of our Lord the Spirit deigned to assist its production by the means of two characteristics of Christendom—exchange and conversion. As was said earlier, co-inherence had been the very pattern of Christendom; we were not to be merely inheritors but " brethren and fellows and co-inheritors of the name of salvation." And as Augustine had taught that that co-inherence stretched back to Adam, so Christendom had carried it forward and beyond into all relationships, up to the last point of the active blessed. The invocation of Saints had arisen from it, and the practice of indulgences had defined it in action. The first Indulgences had been declared to the early Crusaders; all temporal penalties of sin were remitted to those who fought. This was but a method, and two steps were still to be taken before the whole superb and dangerous knowledge became defined. In the thirteenth century Alexander of Hales defined the Treasury of Merits, and in 1343 the doctrine was accepted by Clement VI. In 1457 Calixtus III formally declared that the exercise of such powers was applicable beyond this world, so mightily had the organization become conscious of itself. It was indeed rather a new manner of measurement and a ratification which was then proclaimed, since prayer had always been believed to be effective in the Divine Will. But an accurate method of exchange was then presented to the faithful; by doing *this, that* would be achieved. Indulgences were " applicable to the souls in purgatory." Acts of love could be, definitely and locally, offered to the dead; the visible and invisible worlds co-inhered in that grace; the great means of substituted love became as visible on earth as it was in heaven. Money was, on earth, a means of artificial exchange, and could be, now, a means of the art of heavenly exchange—money given in repentance, in faith, in love. As the intention was struck into act—" as the money chinks in the box "—the effect was achieved—" the soul springs from purgatory."

It was, however, the chink of the money that too much deflected attention. The Lord Leo X, acting within his Pontifical rights and (by definition) offering the faithful a new opportunity of concrete and calculated exchange, and no less profitable to all souls concerned for being concrete and calculated, issued a special Indulgence. That he wished to use the money obtained for building St. Peter's was the Lord Leo's own responsibility, and his own business how much piety went to the building. The arrangement made, however, did rather savour of simony. A particularly brilliant financial idea occurred to someone—to Leo, to a Cardinal, to the Archbishop of Mainz, or (since God frequently confounds his own works by the most unlikely instruments) to some clerk in the train of the Archbishop or in the Papal Treasury at Rome who never perhaps lived to see the catastrophic results of his moment of commercial intelligence. The Archbishop of Mainz, Albert of Hohenzollern, had just been elected. He was not yet of canonical age to hold a bishopric, and he already held two others—he was Archbishop of Magdeburg and Administrator of Halberstadt. He offered the Pontiff ten thousand ducats for concession and confirmation. It was agreed that the money should be advanced by the great banking house of Fugger and paid to the Pope, who should then allocate to Albert, for the Fuggers, the receipts from the Indulgences. The Fuggers took over the management of the sale, arranged for commercial travellers —that is, preachers—sent agents with them to check the takings, and shared the results with the young Archbishop. Such was the idea, such was the arrangement. Unfortunately whoever thought of it dropped a lighted match into that unknown cellar of man's mind which contains the heavily dynamic emotions known as " faith " and " works."

The sale was to begin from 1 April, 1515. Some six or seven years before, the second element in the approaching crisis had been prepared. A young monk of twenty-five or so, older by a year or two than the involved Archbishop of Mainz, had found himself involved in another desire. His name was Luther; he was an Augustinian. Our Lord the Spirit permitted him to follow Augustine in Augustine's primary and continuous desire and to experience conversion. He laboured for it; he suffered austerities, he read, he studied, he prayed, he agonized. He toiled under the teaching of William of Occam that salvation is (after grace) a matter of the will. It is conceivable that it was the later scolastics who were antipathetic to Luther; he liked Athanasius and read Augustine with passion. But all his duties, the sacrament and the solitary studies, brought him no help. The great organization of redemption coiled round him and his soul was in despair. " When I looked for Christ it seemed to me as if I saw the devil." A thousand years earlier the universe for Augustine had shifted its centre in a garden; it did so suddenly now for Luther—it is said, on the *Scala Sancta* at Rome. In a passion of hopeless revolt against the will he had read the *Epistle to the Romans*; he remembered suddenly " The just shall live by faith." He remembered; he stood up; all things swung into order. " The just shall live by faith." Faith.

It was not primarily the scholastics, however, but Aristotle who, he felt, had misled him and more enraged him—" that ridiculous and injurious blasphemer." " My soul longs for nothing so ardently as to expose and publicly shame that Greek buffoon, who like a spectre has befooled the Church." Aristotle had done nothing that he had needed, and brought no peace. He wrote to another Augustinian " You say with Israel : ' Peace, peace,' and there is no peace; say rather with Christ : ' Cross, cross,' and there is no cross. For the cross is no more a cross once you say joyously : ' Blessed cross, there is no tree like thee . . .' " It was this experience which was setting him slowly at odds with his world—as for instance with the five thousand relics which the Elector Frederick of Saxony kept in the Castle Church at Wittenburg, and with the theologians who stressed the language of " works."

In 1517 a travelling preacher of Indulgences came near to Wittenburg; the Elector of Saxony had forbidden the sale to take place in his dominions, and the frontier was not crossed. The preacher was a Dominican named Tetzel; his work was assisted by the Archbishop Albert who had announced in a declaration of the benefit of the Indulgences that—at any rate for those applicable to the souls in Purgatory : " Nor is it necessary for those who contribute to the fund for this purpose to be contrite or to confess." Tetzel preached enthusiastically; his hearers bought. In the miracle of co-inherence there is no reason to suppose that the Indulgences were not effectual for all the glad and aspiring ghosts to whom they were offered. But of that assistance offered by the Church militant to the Church in purification the earthly scandal was an unfortunate result.

The tales told of Tetzel would be incredible were it not that the thing happening is so often more like a fable than the thing supposed. Luther, writing to the Archbishop, said that people reported Tetzel as having preached that " there was no sin so great that it would not be absolved thereby, even if, as they say, taking an impossible example, a man should violate the mother of God. They believe that indulgences free them from all penalty and guilt." It is unlikely that Tetzel meant to commit himself to the heretical belief that an Indulgence could free from *guilt*, as distinguished from the penalty. But it is not impossible that the crowd of German listeners understood him so, nor that his crude phrases may have risen to wild extravagances of rhetoric, carried off precisely by his choice of the impossible image of the *anthropotokos* to particularize. Conceive a Shakespearian clown agitating for piety remote from the quiet studies of theologians, and the situation is credible. Tetzel afterwards denied most of the charges, believe him or not.

Even the broad taste of the times was a little shocked. Tetzel and the Fuggers' agents together were a little too much. The combination of a reckless oratory and a careful calculation were a little too—Shakespearian. Even so nothing might have happened if Luther had not been converted, " in the twinkling of an eye," to faith. He had known the Spirit. It had not entered his head to believe anything but that the organization of the Church was at bottom actuated by the same Spirit. Yet his parishioners were full of the Indulgences and not at all full of contrition. Contrition was not, in that age, a mark of the Church. But it certainly had been a mark of Luther. He had been delivered into assurance. Neither contrition nor assurance, but an obscene parody of both, seemed to him encouraged by the click-clack of the money and the mechanism of grace. The Machine had got out of control, through the faults of the hierarchy. He protested. He protested in the correct academic fashion. He put up theses for dispute; they were not extreme. He allowed " the apostolic truth of indulgences "; he said that " papal pardons are not to be despised." Nor did he produce any antagonistic theological doctrine. He protested, in fact, on the other side little that the calm thought of Christendom would not have admitted. But he did seem to reflect, if not, as Erasmus said later, on " the crown of the Pope and the bellies of the monks," at least on the prestige of the Pope and the profits of the preachers. The news of the protest spread; it reached the Lord Leo, who was good-natured, tolerant, amused. " A drunken German monk! he will think differently when he is sober!" Alas, the inebriation was deep; Luther had drunk of the intoxicating Blood.

Even now it seems astonishing that one moment, as against so many others, should have set fire to so much. Luther was neither a great mystic nor a great theologian. He might have found all that he ever found in a thousand orthodox doctors. He denied nothing, at least in the beginning, that a thousand orthodox doctors would not have denied. But two things combined against peace and reconciliation; the first was the immediate alignment of forces, the second was certain particular conversions permitted or encouraged by the Spirit.

The alignment of forces tended to be upon that old frontier of dispute, the argument on faith and works. It has often been regarded as a technicality of theology; in fact, of course, it is a matter like most theology—of everyday life. It is a matter of understanding and approach; it is almost a matter of style. Do we do best to think of achieving what we can by ourselves? or to rely upon something not ourselves? And if either, how far? and with what modifications? In such a matter as the desirability of loving A, do we leave it to X to love A? or do we try and love A directly? which is the best method for developing a pure style of love? We all know the deplorable false styles, the styles which say with intolerable arrogance " Oh well, I do what I can," or with an equally intolerable smirk " Oh well, of course, it isn't I that do it, but Something Else " (and if the Something Else is named the effect is no better). How do we become honest? and what kind of works does " faith " in love involve? Co-inherence is not finished with when it is named; how then do we best co-inhere?

High abstractions—upon which every minute of personal life depends! What is the nature of love? Christendom had felt how helpless man was to do anything; Paul and Augustine, to name no others, had become witnesses to *that*. You are no nearer being love because you have done acts of love. But are acts of love then of no account? Much every way, so long as you do not claim them for yours. But can I then not exist as action in love? Yes; you exist precisely, at fullest, in the acts which, most intensely, are not yours. And apart from them? Oh apart from them you are corrupt, lost, perishing everlastingly. Your acts are only from the fullness of the treasury of the all-meritorious love of God.

So, roughly, the Faith party; the Works took another, and parallel, line. You exist in those acts—yes; it is up to you to produce them. No one and nothing can produce them except you; unless you do, they will be everlastingly and eternally lost. They are of intense value; their value is such that they are not only applicable to the present situation but to all situations. They affect those dead long since and those yet unborn, as you are affected by the deeds of love of those not yet born or dead long since. All the sacraments are communications of love to all—through you. They at least are certain where so much is uncertain. Act then; act now; act, you. Work while it is called day. Without you and your acts—so marvellously has he limited himself that you may be co-inheritor with him—the acts of Love himself are not yet full.

The alternating stresses were reconcilable enough—in the hearts of the saints, the rhythms of Dante, or anyone's ordinary experience. Along both those parallel roads the columns of Christendom moved to take the kingdom of heaven by storm. But if the columns paused, quarrelled, turned hostile, faced each other, dug trenches along the ways? " The intellect," said Luther, " is the Devil's whore." She may be, at least, the mistress of a passionate emotion, or she may indulge her own sensuality. But, to be fair to her, it is not only self-indulgence which drives her into controversies. Something has, in this world, to be *said*. It was all very well for the Incarnate Glory to refrain from defining his gospel, but he left the task to his disciples, and all the infallibilities have not yet succeeded in making it very much plainer. St. Paul, it seems, was right; only the operation of " faith " succeeds.

At that moment there was, on the one side, a very high intellectual tradition, discovered by first-rate minds but then administered by fifth-rate. On the other side was a first-hand experience, preached largely by second-hand. On both sides were the rag-tag and bobtail of religion, and also the multitudes of the uncomprehending good. Between them were the humanists, the unfortunate intellectuals.

There was an unsatisfactory interview between Luther and the Papal Legate at Augsburg. There was a disputation at Leipzig, where Luther committed himself to the even more extreme (but ancient) view that General Councils could err and had erred. The princes of Germany, a little put about by a tax that Leo proposed to lay on the states, for a Crusade—about which everyone was very doubtful—were either luke-warm or hostile to the Italianate Roman See. In 1518 it became evident that Leo and Luther had each decided that the other was Antichrist. The Bull of Excommunication was issued in June; Luther in August replied with a volume on the Baby-lonish Captivity of the Church. The mitred splendours and the rituals of glory were beginning to seem to him very much like the pageanted gods of Assyria, and that fatal dream of a simple gospel was rising like a marsh-light over the too-soon-bloody swamp of Europe. Luther wrote to Erasmus, more or less suggesting an alliance. Erasmus replied much as Matthew Arnold might have replied to Wesley. He did not think either crowns or bellies worth war, but if war came he knew he would be found with the Roman See. But some of the younger Humanists went over—notably, the almost equally quiet-loving Philip Melanchthon, who thus prepared for himself (like Newman later) a future of spiritual peace and temporal distress.

By 1520 bonfires—of books, so far—were taking place. The Papalists burnt Luther's and the Lutheran's retaliated. Among the fires there appeared a fresh figure—the figure of the new Emperor Charles V. He had no extreme passion for humanism, though he admired it. He had no use at all for mystical conversion. He acknowledged the Papacy, and he had a personal intention to see that the Pope fitted in with his politics. He wished to restore the power of the Holy Roman Empire, and to be himself the Holy Roman Emperor. He was young, remote, practical, orthodox, and firm. He had no intention of assenting to heresy. Yet he was the first European sovereign who was compelled to exclude orthodoxy as a fundamental necessity in his subordinate sovereigns. He began in 1521 with the Diet of Worms. He was driven to compromise—*cujas regio ejus religio*. Luther at Worms said " I can no other "; it was magnificent, but it was not politics.

After Worms Luther was secluded for some time in the Wartburg; he was there from May 1521 to March 1522. The dates recall the second condition which prolonged the split through the centuries. For from March 1522 to January 1523 Ignatius Loyola was also living in seclusion and devotion —but he at the cave of Manresa in Spain. In 1534, as a result of his retirement Luther was able to publish the German translation of the Bible. In the same year Ignatius with six companions took the vows. Among the companions was Francis Xavier, once a lecturer on Aristotle, converted and indoctrinated by Ignatius. In the same year another young classical scholar, a Frenchman who had published in 1532, with much applause, a commentary on Seneca's *De Clementia* (strange choice!), and had been living since in seclusion at Angoulême, also after conversion, composed a small treatise on the primal doctrines of Christianity. His name was John Calvin, and the book was the first draft of the *Institutes of the Christian Religion*. The German Bible, the Jesuits, the *Institutes*—all in one year. And Luther, Ignatius, Xavier, Calvin—the dates of their births are important, but those other dates of conversion are much more important. In that great age of *Homo*, with its magnificences of scholarship, architecture, art, exploration, war, its transient graces and terrene glories, it pleased our Lord the Spirit violently to convulse these souls with himself. Grace seized on those strategic centres for its own campaign. It struck suddenly outward, as its most divine way is—since the wise Pharisee collapsed outside Damascus—and now in a German, a Frenchman, a Spaniard—and many others after them. It had done so, often enough, in the Middle Ages, as since; its business is always to restore contrition to man. But now, when contrition, admitted as a theory, had largely disappeared as a fact, it renewed contrition. The awful conflict opened with those separate vigils of conflict. Contrition had been left, by the Archbishop of Mainz in one set of indulgences, to the souls in purgatory, and he was technically correct. But the result was that, in the other set of indulgences, for those living on earth, the need of contrition could hardly be stressed. The Rites of the Church, however, even in that age of *Homo,* invoked Immanuel. Her governors celebrated them but did not preach their conditions—nor Repentance, the greatest condition (save Faith and Charity) of all. They left it, at best, to be presupposed, and what was presupposed the Spirit gave the Church again—or gave her Lord through her. They had professed contrition for their own purposes; they received contrition for his—" good measure, pressed down and running over." The champions of it and of its assurance—assurance by experience, assurance by belief—sprang into action. That they came as they did—hostile, militant, complete— was due precisely to the condition of sin in which Christendom had found itself and to the redemption which everlastingly works within her.

The tumult passed, inevitably, from souls to minds; minds commanded bodies; bodies took to weapons. The Religious Wars opened as formulation began. It centred at first on those old recurrent questions of the will, and the will in relation to grace, and grace in relation to the system. The great fundamental dogmas of the Nature of Christ remained, in general, formally undisturbed. The Renascence had not attacked them; it had not been particularly aware of them.

But it had been acutely aware of man's will, and of the glorious manifestations of man's will. In France and in Spain a more ancient experiment was again begun. Calvin and Loyola, cavalry commanders of the Spirit in the new campaign, sought also to discover man's will. But they sought its discovery in its supreme moment of self-destruction; they desired to compel it to say " My Eros is crucified." The same word sprang in both— *exercitus,* exercise, drill. *The Exercises* was the title of Loyola's manual; "this life is an exercise," wrote Calvin. That those two masters should have been opposed was, humanly speaking, tragic. They were both children of Christendom, and of medieval Christendom, and at that a medieval Christendom illuminated by the earlier Fathers. They both maintained passionately the authority of the Church. "We believe the Church," wrote Calvin, " in order to have a certain assurance that we are members of it. For thus our salvation rests on firm and solid foundation, so that it cannot fall into ruin, though the whole fabric of the world should be dissolved," and he went on to quote Augustine. To say that Calvin was influenced by Augustine is a meiosis; Augustine is invoked on almost every page of the great *Institutes.* He says of him, in speaking of the great doctrine of Election, "I need no words but his," and again, " I shall not hesitate to confess with Augustine : ' The Will of God is the necessity of things.' "

It was this complete necessity which the genius of Calvin attempted to restore as the only basis of the universal Church. He desired to attribute *all* initiative to God, and to show that all things existed only according to the will of that initiative. "Calvinism asks, with Lutheranism, that most pregnant of all questions : what shall I do to be saved? and answers it as Lutheranism answers it. But the great question that presses upon it is, How shall God be glorified?"[3] How but by acknowledging that in him alone is all decision? in him alone all necessity? in him alone all destination? He asserts,

[3] *Calvin and Calvinism,* Benjamin Warfield.

and we can but consent; we do it of necessity and yet volun-
tarily. We have chosen necessity, and that necessity elects
as it will, some to salvation, some to damnation.

Augustine had said almost as much, and if it were not for
Augustine's sweep of style even the " almost " would be
exaggerated. But his great phrases soar above the very
definitions they carry; Calvin quotes from him " We do not
find grace by liberty, but liberty by grace." All the psychological doctors of the Mystical Way had assented. Calvin
attempted to formulate that experience. But no such dogma
has ever been satisfactory to the Church that does not involve
free lives mutually co-inhering, and necessity and freedom
(dare one say?) mutually co-inhering. In the Crucifixion of
Messias necessity and freedom had mutually crucified each
other, and both (as if in an exchanged life) had risen again.
Freedom existed then because it must; necessity because it
could. But Calvin crucified Adam upon Jesus; " Men are to
be taught indeed that the Divine Benignity is free to all who
seek it, without any exception." *But* " none begin to seek it
but those who have been inspired by the Divine Grace."
All initiative is from God.

Men have not, for the most part, been able to bear the
terrible paradox of Calvin, and they have pretended that
Calvinism is (intellectually) much easier than it is. They
have in fact (though generally from mean motives of ignorance and dislike) brought it under the condemning sentence of
Loyola, " We ought not to speak of grace at such length
and so vehemently as to give rise to that poisonous teaching
which takes away free will." But then Ignatius had a great
advantage; he did not conceive himself to be laying down the
first principles of the Christian religion, but only founding
an Order. He was no Calvin or Aquinas. He only sought to
teach the soul to discover the personal will in its moment of
destruction; he only immolated on a superhuman individual
devotion the glory of the Renascence. He presumed man's
personal freewill in heaven but he enlisted his followers to the
loss of it on earth; so much so that the ecclesiastical author-

ities checked and modified the more extreme of his phrases. The Constitution of his Society suggested a subordination to superiors of a more utter kind than Rome was prepared to allow. Even the famous phrase about black and white—" we ought always to believe that what seems to us white is black, if the hierarchical Church so define it "—may allow of some discussion, though it is difficult to see in the end what other conclusion can be formally reached. What is clear is that here also contrition, election, annihilation, were living states. Newman defined the chief characteristic of Ignatius to be " prudence "—intelligence of the spirit. He, more than Calvin, exhibited (if he did not more believe) the doctrine of exchange.

Both those great men renewed the word. The sermon came again into its own, but more extremely under Calvin than under Ignatius. Of all the incomprehensibilities of that difficult time perhaps the most incomprehensible to us is the passion of the Reformed for sermons. That men and women should wish to sit and *listen,* to do nothing but sit and listen, for hours together, is unbelievable to us, and we explain it by thinking that they were listening for heresies, listening in fear of the power of the ministers, or listening in terrible delight to hear their enemies denounced to hell, and no doubt all these things sooner or later came in, but not one was the main thing; no, the main thing was simply the spoken word, the energy and accuracy of the spoken word, the salvation communicated in the sacrament of the spoken word. Those congregations returned almost to the " speaking with tongues " of an earlier day, though this speaking did not need interpretation, for the interpretation and the speaking were one. They returned to Pentecost and the Spirit manifesting by tongues. And besides the sermons there were other tongues —tongues of psalms and hymns and spiritual songs, but especially of psalms. Initiative of God, breath of the Spirit of God, words moulded by the fiery Spirit from the burning hearts of his elect. " Praise him upon the loud cymbals; praise him upon the well-tuned cymbals." The cymbals were the voices; their sound went over the earth, and as the wars grew darker the noise grew fiercer. "Let God arise, and let his enemies be scattered." Calvinist and Jesuit alike gave themselves to martyrdom, and the secular authorities laboured to keep up with the intellectual rage that lit the fires, fires round the stake or fires under the gallows, fires of interior contrition catching and spreading, and changed into those other fires which should destroy the ungodly and make their very flesh the burning gate of hell for their souls, or image in their castrated bodies the sterile miseries of everlasting loss. "Let God arise, and let his enemies be scattered." The single spiritual conflicts of those great souls, those powers taking the Kingdom by violence, and radiating their violence outward through Christendom, opened into a general temporal conflict. Noise and austerity went with them; their high rage of righteousness drew armies after them, and the agony of a wailing continent replied to their silent agonies of attention. The real reformation, of which the Reformation generally so-called is but a small part, advanced. But as it came—" let God arise and let his enemies be scattered "—it too much lost the thoughts of co-inherent love. Contrition indeed was renewed—but not for its own day, only for the day before yesterday.

CHAPTER VIII

THE QUALITY OF DISBELIEF

There was present, therefore, by half-way through the six-teenth century, in all the nations of Europe, to whatever Profession they adhered, the thing that had been regarded through all the Middle Ages as the worst danger—heresy. The effort to impose, as a preliminary to the great experiment of salvation, the necessary conditions of that experiment had resulted in the conditions, from any point of view, being militantly contradicted. In every country a minority of " heretics " could be and was aided by a majority of " heretics " in another country. From being a threat heresy had become a continuous event—and this was true of the Reformed and Protesting Churches as of the Roman. That the event could finally endure was not supposed. It was not imagined that various formations in Christendom could maintain themselves side by side—in spite of the evidence to the contrary offered by the existence of the Eastern Churches. The Eastern Churches had always been remote, and since the fall of Con-stantinople had become even more remote; they were sub-ordinate under Islam. That the existence of those various Western formations, and their controversies, could become irrelevant to political and social life was even less imaginable. Heresies, however huge, were imagined to be temporary, and therefore all agreements and treaties with them were also imagined to be temporary—as we see they are to-day among the extreme supporters of our different ideologies. A man, it is felt, cannot be expected to keep faith with something which contradicts and destroys the whole nature of faith and of life. " No faith with heretics " is not an ecclesiastical rule; it is a natural and inevitable human emotion. To make a frontier agreement with a nation of cannibals cannot really forbid an intention to interfere with the cannibals as soon or as much as is convenient; we cannot seriously be expected to let the cannibals against all basis of good go on eating their aged parents. It is inhuman, and with the inhuman there can be no treaty. This is the difficulty of toleration; it is also the objection to toleration. So, in the sixteenth century, the religious armies felt. Years were to go by before the secular governments were compelled by their own eventual impotency to recognize that other beliefs existed and would continue to exist. At first, and for a hundred years or so, strong efforts were made to prevent their existence. It is arguable that the one point which decided that those efforts should fail and that a different state of things should come into being was the life —unexpectedly prolonged—and the beliefs—unexpectedly ambiguous—of Elizabeth of England.

But before that new state of things came into being, and before its rising power can be traced, there is one life which stood, as it were, as deep within the commonalty of holiness as the new movement shifted from the commonalty of doctrine. In 1542 there was born, in that Spain which had produced Loyola and, a few years later, Teresa, a certain Juan de Yepes, called John of the Cross. He died in 1591, and his life seems as if it were the compensation for the glory of the Renascence Popes and the cost of the recovery of the Papacy. Saints enough had sprung up on all sides under the strain of that century, and no greater constellation than surrounded the Roman See. But John of the Cross seems of another nature even than those. The combination of his own interior method and the method by which in the universe God acceded to his desire—these, combined with the high crisis of contrition during which he lived, draw up in him the appearance of a vicarious sacrifice, and set him, or should set him, beyond the reach of any easy admiration. He pursued strongly the Way of the Rejection of Images, the Negative Way. He wrote : " If a man wishes to be sure of the road he travels on, he must close his eyes and walk in the dark." " There is only

one method, that which makes empty." He allowed indeed
to "beginners" the use of sensitive and tangible apprehen-
sions, but these were later to be repudiated—understanding,
memory, and will "in the matter of their operations." The
great Dionysian metaphysic became to him a close and most
intimate experience, the Nothing became the All; and his
sayings have to be interpreted in this sense or they become
dangerous. As, for instance, the maxim : "Speak disparagingly of thyself, and contrive that others may do so
too "—which avoids delicately an encouragement in others of
a lack of intelligence or a lack of charity, since it is hardly
to be supposed that John of the Cross himself would have
consented to "speak disparagingly" of others. But the word
there has itself almost lost its exact meaning; the image of
"others" has faded; there is left but a formulated wish
to "contrive" the destruction of the image of oneself. The
end of the Way has never been put better : "In the awakening of the Bridegroom in the perfect soul, all is perfect because
he effects it all himself. . . . In this awakening, as of one
aroused from sleep and drawing breath, the soul feels the
breathing of God."

It is reported that during his first Mass John had prayed
never to commit a mortal sin, and "to suffer, during this
life, the penance for all those faults which, in his weakness,
he might have committed, if God were not sustaining him."
The rest of his life suggests that God took him at his word,
and made his word far more fruitful than even he could then
have supposed. For he did not suffer abuse and imprison-
ment from the world or from Islam but from the priests and
Fathers of his own Church. He was persecuted by the
Church for the good of the Church; they thought so, and
so (in another sense) it was. His body received the effects of
corruption; it was full of abscesses and sores; he suffered
extreme pain. It is reported also that the pus from the sores
gave out a good smell; women said it was "as if we had
been handling flowers." Out of the mistaken, though well-
intended, disputes and separations among his superiors, out of

his own passion for the loss of all, there came the experience of union and, it seems, some sort of transmutation of the flesh. He was, then and there, an epigram of Christendom. (And even he, towards the end, was encouraged to remember that he liked asparagus; our Lord the Spirit is reluctant to allow either of the two great Ways to flourish without some courtesy to the other.)

But that was solitary; the other movement was communal. In the first opening of the wars—the Wars of Religion in Germany and France, of Revolt in the Netherlands, of the seas between Spain and England, of the Thirty Years War in the Empire, and the lesser but related crises in Scotland, in Scandinavia, in Switzerland, there was everywhere a belief in and hope for ultimate military and metaphysical victory. That hope and belief were soon complicated by other causes, social and economic; and, as in the Netherlands, Catholics and Calvinists sometimes found themselves strange tent-fellows and treaty-fellows. Economics confused the process of the Reformation as they had been partly responsible for the beginning of the Reformation. But the general dreams of things to come were still dictated by the subconscious habits of a thousand years and encouraged by the discovery of the energetic habits of our Lord the Spirit at all times. Compromise was unthinkable, and toleration had to be a necessity before it could be a virtue. In fact, as a virtue it does not yet exist, though we once thought it did. For our fathers became bored and miserable and decadent through their incessant killing, and we, the children of that killing, supposed ourselves to be convinced of charity, when, in truth, we only shuddered still at the memory of blood.

In a kingdom of the West, soon after Luther had been shaken by his parishioners' satisfaction with indulgences, a moment of variation had also appeared. But there it took its rise not from the New Birth of the Spirit but from a horror of the flesh. The King of England had married, at the will of his father and somewhat against his own, the widow of his elder brother. Such a marriage had needed a dispensation

from the Roman See before it could be effected, and it was
well known that serious and prolonged delay had occurred
in Rome before it was decided that the dispensation could be
granted. England and the King of England very greatly
desired that the King should have a male heir, to establish
the dynasty and to prevent any recurrence of the recent Civil
Wars. It was hoped that God would bless the marriage with
a son or sons. The King had intercourse with his wife. She
conceived. She conceived five times—three of the children
were born dead; one lived three months; one lived—ill
and sickly, but it lived. It was a girl. God seemed to exhibit
to the King the visible taunts of his displeasure.

The King had a simple religious feeling, a real but limited
theological intelligence, and a strong tendency to superstition—that is, to supposing that the good or bad chances
of things signified the immediate pleasure or displeasure of
Almighty God. Henry did not believe that all luck was
good; nor was he singular in that; the age largely supported
him. The recurrent outrage of intimate death destroyed his
hopes and unsettled his mind; and indeed the physiological
strain of turning again to the bed of Katherine of Aragon,
with the five times frustrated (and how frustrated!) hope of
an heir might have tried stronger nerves. It was a cruel and
a brutal time; Henry was callous enough even in such an age.
Had he had a profoundly affectionate or a profoundly moral
nature he might have governed himself in another way. He
had not. But he did not blame the Queen or himself; he
blamed the dispensation. It was obvious that the Roman
See had no power to grant it; there had been a mistake. He
desired the mistake corrected. He had fallen in love with a
lady whom he wished now, legally and canonically, to marry;
the more so that she would not yield herself on any other
terms. But that was only an additional—if the most sensa-
tional—incentive; he also desired, as he always had, a legal and
canonical heir. God had sent him only dead babies for heirs—
and one girl living but likely to die. He could not understand
how any man could deny him his desire or refuse him his

rights. He opened, seriously and conscientiously, the question of the Nullity of the marriage.

It was discussed and re-discussed. Rome sent a Legate with powers. At the moment when judgment was about to be given in England, his powers were suspended and the whole case was recalled to Rome. The King was in a fury. He felt he had been cheated—which was more or less true. An abyss of treachery opened before him—treachery not merely to himself but to the obvious will of Almighty God. The Pope was false to God and to him. He turned to the English ecclesiastical authorities who, immediately and probably sincerely, determined that the marriage had been null and void. The King, perfectly convinced that the behaviour of the Pope exhibited an unheard-of meanness, hypocrisy, and turpitude, pressed his denunciation of the Roman See. Within two years the whole ecclesiastical organization of England—except for a score of martyrs—had explicitly renounced, apparently with surprisingly little sense of doing anything unusual, the primacy and jurisdiction of Rome. But then it was only a century or a little more, as historical time goes, that they had had to decide which of two equal figures, on equal evidence, represented the primacy and jurisdiction of Rome.

The contending doctrines of the Continent played, then and for long thereafter, very little part in the affair. There were Lutherans in England, but they had not a great deal of missionary success. The few orthodox martyrs did not suffer for any great Catholic doctrines—apart from the Primacy. England could not compete with Germany, but neither could she compete with Spain. Sir Thomas More was begged by high ecclesiastics to submit, as was Luther; and the later demand of the Western Rebels that they should not be made to communicate more than once a year would have been almost as repugnant to Loyola as to Luther. The Church in England underwent, in the next thirty years, a number of shocks. She was threatened with Calvinism at one time and reconciled to Rome at another. But she was not overthrown by another Church, old or new. For a long time everything that happened happened within her. She continued to operate formally, and she retained a continual spiritual awareness of herself. The idea that there was at any time any break in the steady outward hierarchical succession or the use of the Rites or the repetition of the Creeds or the attendance in the churches is abandoned. Nor is it tenable that any of the successors of the earlier clergy supposed themselves to be doing anything against the intention of Christ; on the contrary, they all imagined themselves to be passionately restoring the intention of Christ. The denunciation of her depends on the view that this is not sufficient; that they must (to retain power) have intended to do secondarily as well as primarily what Christ intended; and that He withdrew from the Sacraments in which not His presence but a particular mode of His presence was denied. The examinations of Cranmer at Oxford before his martyrdom exhibit the delicacy of the problem. But that it is delicate does not, of course, mean that it is insoluble. The single un-doubted fact is that between the " slight column " of Calvin counter-weighing the ocean-mass of Trent, the Church of England pursued her odd (but not, for that, necessarily less sacred) way, still aware of herself as related to all the past, and to the ceremonial presences of Christ.

To attribute the dead children of the princess of Aragon to the decision of the Holy Spirit would be to fall into King Henry's error, and to attribute to secondary causes the intention of the First Cause. But at least it may be said that a kind of fatality hung over the marriage, and a kind of fatality also hangs over the corresponding fact that Henry's daughter by Anne Boleyn was what she was. As if the Spirit rebuked the assumption that our results are His results, the result of Henry's pious conviction of sin, combined with Anne's determination on marriage, was a woman whose temperament was opposed to all assumptions. No one really knows what Elizabeth of England believed. She had kept vigil against secret and public enemies too long, through all her first five-and-twenty years, ever to be able to reveal her heart. She had a vivid sense of this world's goods and this world's spectacles; except when she went hysterical with rage and frustration, she hated blood. When the Pope and King Philip of Spain separately offered to give her back her throne if she would first admit that she had no right to it, she was not holy enough to bring herself to do so. She would have had, in that case, to admit that the woman who had the right was Mary of Scotland, and this she was determined not to do. She was determined to keep Mary out, and she succeeded. But also she kept Mary alive for seventeen years, and the King of France wondered at it. Hardly any other ruler in Christendom would have done both; the assassination of Elizabeth herself was discussed at the Spanish council-tables.

The ruler most like Elizabeth was just across the Narrow Seas, Catharine de Medici, Queen-Mother of France. They were dissimilar enough, yet a similarity exists. They were both confronted by nations which tended to disunion, by civil wars or threats of civil war. They both wanted quiet times and enjoyments—for themselves and, as far as possible, for their people. They both hated the religious raging of the populace; or, in Elizabeth's phrase to Catharine, " that metamorphosis where the head is removed to the foot, and the heels hold the highest place." They found the dancing heels more fantastical and fanatical than the heads, certainly than their two heads. They both broke under pressure and in a passion of nerves; they both half-regretted it—Elizabeth when she had Mary Stuart put to death, Catharine when she gave the signal for the Bartholomew. Catharine was inside, and Elizabeth was outside, the now limited Roman system; but both of them would have read with relief and satisfaction the sentence engraved at S. Maria Maggiore at Trent when the Council had finished its sittings : " Here the Holy Spirit spoke for the last time "—" *postremum Spiritus Sanctus oracula effudit.*"[1]

[1] *The Inner History of the Great Schism*, G. J. Jordan.

The Churches were defined and militant; the States were torn and harassed. By natural processes the States proceeded to eject the trouble from their blood. The breath of a new repugnancy was drawn first by Elizabeth and Catharine. But even before that the contending Religions had been driven to a reluctant compromise in the Confession of Augsburg in 1530, and had concluded on *cujus regio ejus religio*. It was unsatisfactory, for both sides believed that the Holy Spirit had spoken to them, if not finally, at least with a definite finality, since finality was in the nature of His utterances. Nor (obviously) could He make peace with what was opposed to Him. It might almost be said that Elizabeth and Catharine both felt that, at a pinch, He could. Catharine had probably few uncertainties accompanying her accepted central certainty; Elizabeth may have had more—if indeed her hidden centre was not itself uncertain. "Fear God, serve the King, and be a good fellow to the rest," she wrote colloquially to the securely Protestant Burghley in one of his fits of gloom, tears and desperation. She was not herself much of a good fellow to the Jesuits, nor even to the Puritans; yet persistently it was her dream. Under all her diplomacy she felt an injustice in the Catholic opposition. "Your chief pastor pronounced sentence against me while I was in my mother's womb," she said to the Roman priests. It was that unborn child she all her life defended and justified, and there obscurely she believed in God. She died, as she had lived, alone.

The great renewal of Contrition had taken place about 1518-34. It culminated round about 1550-60. The pontificate of Paul IV reformed, with incredible speed and scope, the conventional abuses of the Roman Church; it is almost the supreme example of reform in history. Luther had died in 1546; Loyola in 1556; Calvin in 1564. The Council of Trent formulated the Roman doctrine as against the rest. Elizabeth was excommunicated and formally deposed; the military and naval effort to carry out the sentence to the advantage of the King of Spain, failed. In 1588 the Armada was foiled and the Elizabethan methods were left to work. In 1593 King Henry of Navarre submitted to the Roman Church, became Henry IV of France, and pacified the country by using both Roman Catholic and Huguenot gentlemen in his government: " Paris "—and still more *" la paix "*—*" vaut bien une messe."* Elizabeth might—and almost did—say that in similar circumstances; just as Henry IV might well have bidden his minister fear God, serve the King, and be a good fellow to the rest. " Every peasant shall have a chicken in his pot on Sunday," he is reported to have said; he left the peasants to go where they would on Sunday otherwise. There were fewer chickens and fewer peasants than there had been before the wars. A little later Richelieu, minister to King Henry's son, assisted the transformation of the religious conflict into a political. He called in the Protestant " Lion of the North," the Swedish King Gustavus Adolphus, against the Empire. He substituted the Franco-German crisis for the Pelagian-Augustinian crisis. Gustavus was defeated and slain by the Emperor's General Wallenstein. But Wallenstein himself fell out of favour with his devout Imperial master partly because he was inclined to treat creeds a little lightly. The secular governments, even when ecclesiastics like Richelieu dominated them, began to forget metaphysics. The Thirty Years War ended in 1648. Of the concluding treaties a distinguished Roman Catholic historian has written: " The Treaties of 1648 really mark the end of an epoch, or rather they are a definite sign that the age in which the Catholic Church, through its head the Pope, was a recognized force in the public life of Europe, had finally come to an end. After more than a thousand years the State was once more to transact its business as though the Church did not exist."[2]

It was true also of the States in which the Reformed and Protesting Churches existed. The operation of faith was not a matter of which secular governments proposed to take much cognizance, unless and until it became inconvenient to them. At the same time the organization existed every-

[2] *A Popular History of the Church,* Fr. Philip Hughes.

where, and there were exceptions. This result was not surprising. Contrition and the taking of faith seriously had meant untold suffering, had meant fierce and continual horrors, within nations and between nations. Something general and very deep in man awoke to revolt, of which Elizabeth and Catharine and Henry of Navarre were the political signs. It may have been mere exhaustion, or perhaps mere humanitarianism (which at such times is seen to have a beauty all its own), which gave it an opportunity. But it rose. It was a quality of spirit, not clarity (though it may involve clarity), not charity (though it may lead to charity). It is a rare thing, and it may be called the quality of disbelief. It is a manner, a temperament, a nature, which may be encouraged or discouraged; it is most particularly not irony, though irony may be an element in it. It is a qualitative mode of belief rather than a quantitative denial of dogma. No doubt, since it is human, it had existed in the Middle Ages, and indeed all through the history of Christendom. But perhaps the best example earlier than the sixteenth century is in the story told of the Renascence notable, Lorenzo Valla. That very distinguished scholar, who had exposed the forgery of the Decretals, came under suspicion of heresy because he preferred Cicero's Latin to that of the Vulgate and indulged himself in a few other intellectual luxuries. The Inquisition at Naples said to him in effect, like the angels in Jerome's dream a thousand years before: "You are no Christian; you are a Ciceronian" It is an example of the old difficulty that what a wise man may say to himself it is rash for lesser men to say to others. They collected Valla and interrogated him; they invited him to state his views. He answered that he believed all that Holy Church believed. He added, with the accuracy of a scholar, that She did not *know*; She believed, and, with her, he. Messer Lorenzo Valla was then a secretary of the King of Spain, in whose dominions Naples was, and his august master caused the process to be quashed. The Popes approved; one invited Valla to Rome; Calixtus III made him a Pontifical Secretary and (most suitably) a Canon of St. John Lateran upon the Caelian Hill—"the Mother and Mistress of all churches."

The answer is an example of this quality of disbelief. It is entirely accurate; it comes straight from the Creed. It covers all the doctrines. It is entirely consistent with sanctity. Yet undoubtedly it also involves as much disbelief as possible; it allows for, it encourages, the sense of agnosticism and the possibility of error. It hints ambiguity—nicely balancing belief and disbelief, qualifying each by the other, and allowing belief only its necessary right proportion of decisiveness.

Such a method has the same dangers as any other; that is, it is quite sound when a master uses it, cheapens as it becomes popular, and is unendurable when it is merely fashionable. So Augustine's predestination was safe with him, comprehensible in Calvin, tiresome in the English Puritans, and quite horrible in the Scottish presbyteries. There is no way of saving these things; even Francis of Assisi has produced, unintentionally, circles of hopeless bathos. All we can hope is that we may, by grace, recover different modes as and when they are most needed. This particular one was needed in the sixteenth and seventeenth centuries. Our Lord the Spirit, having permitted contrition to exist, permitted sheer intelligence to exist; he inspired—one may say so—Montaigne. Montaigne had been born in 1533—in the same year as Elizabeth of England, the year before the German Bible and the *Institutes* and the Jesuit vows—in Gascony, the son of a Roman Catholic father and a mother of Jewish blood and Protestant opinions. In middle life he was used as an intermediary between the House of Guise and the Huguenot Henry of Navarre, for whom he seems to have had a high regard. After 1570 he retired into private life and he died in 1592, after the Armada and before Henry's decision that "*Paris vaut bien une messe.*" He received communion on his death-bed.

He kept orthodoxy all his life, and it was a deliberate orthodoxy; he knew what he was about. "There is no reason," said one of his English admirers, "for disbelieving Montaigne's sincere and conscious orthodoxy in the ecclesiastical sense."[3] On the other hand, another has written that in him "all forms of dogmatism are alike discredited as phases of the same folly of certitude in matters essentially uncertain."[4] Montaigne himself carried on Valla's phrase : " This idea (the Pyrrhonian view) is more surely understood by interrogation : What do I know? which I bear as my motto with the emblem of a pair of scales.' He found two sources of the world's distresses : " Most of the grounds of the world's troubles are matters of grammar," and " The conviction of wisdom is the plague of man. That is why ignorance is so much recommended by our religion, as a fitting element of faith and obedience." Is that ironical? to call it so and not to call it so are alike false. Gibbon in England, two centuries later, touches the note again sometimes in the *Decline,* but then from other sentences we know that, at bottom, he means only to sneer, and so the grand value of the ambiguity is lost. " It is not possible," said Montaigne, " for a man to rise above himself and his humanity;" and again : " We are, I know not how, double in ourselves, so that what we believe we disbelieve, and cannot rid ourselves of what we condemn."

The " double man " of Montaigne is not the same as the " double man " of the unknown Egyptian monk, though at that they are not necessarily opposed. His spirit was not the formula of the substantial spiritual co-inherence, but then Christendom had not been able to get very far with substantial co-inherence, and in 1580 it seemed farther off than ever. Montaigne proposed another kind of co-inherence. He recalled men to the recollection that they began with a hypothesis; that faith—the kind of faith he beheld active round him, which had (it was estimated) killed 800,000 human beings and wrecked nine towns and two hundred and fifty villages—*that* faith had first been a hypothesis and had

[3] *History of French Literature,* George Saintsbury. It is true Dr. Saintsbury was himself orthodox.
[4] *Introduction to Montaigne,* J. G. Robertson. It is true Mr. Robertson was himself agnostic.

been generally translated into the realms of certitude by anger and obstinacy and egotism. Even of profound spiritual experience the sentence that he put up in his library was true: " Men are tormented by their opinions of things, not by the things themselves." Thomas à Kempis had said it in another idiom: " The Holy Ghost has delivered me from a multitude of opinions." Man has always to proceed by hypotheses. But to accept a hypothesis as a hypothesis is precisely to admit that some other possibility may exist. Are we to comment on our own hypothesis in the light of other possibilities? and do not other people exist, holding other hypotheses? and must we not regard their convictions as some kind of " compensation " for our own? must we not be, in that sense at least, a " double man "?

But to defend or to explain that belief-in-disbelief is to weaken it. It was natural—nay, it was supernatural—in Montaigne. He believed in the old human *pietas* of religion, the religion of custom, of good tradition, " of my king and my nurse." But he made a point of *believing* in it; he grew into some state of mind through it; he seems to have dis-armed the soldiers who once raided his house through a serenity and courtesy not unlike St. Francis, though without the quality of shining ecstasy. Anything is possible—even that all things are possible or that nothing is possible. And " when we are angry we defend our proposition the more hotly; we impress it on ourselves and espouse it with greater vehemence and approval than in our cool and calm moments." The history of Christendom itself would have been far happier could we all have remembered *that* rule of intelligence—not to believe a thing more strongly at the end of a bitter argument than at the beginning, not to believe it with the energy of the opposition rather than with one's own. " I can maintain an opinion; I cannot choose one." But if God has revealed one? He Himself can maintain it then; we need not be disturbed. There also " we are, I know not how, double in ourselves."

Montaigne was a gentleman and a man of letters; he was not a theologian or a saint, and to observe him is to run the danger of becoming, or of being accused of becoming, "literary." But Letters have always played a part in Christendom, and though Letters are not and never can be Religion, yet style has had an immense influence on Religion; so much so that it has been held that an increased attention to style would at times have done Religion all the good in the world —this world; the good of any other she already had from heaven. It was chiefly Montaigne's style, as it had been the style of Erasmus and of St. Thomas, which made his writings fashionable in the generations after his own, and made the mind of his " double man " into an influence in France. Unfortunately, as so often happens, the minds of his readers were not the equal of his own, and could not maintain his poise. His duplicity was split; his ambiguity was reduced to irony; and the quality of unbelief with which he believed was extracted and congealed. What Richelieu did politically, the readers of Montaigne did intellectually. National interests and mental relaxations combined to exclude metaphysics from culture. Ritual became nothing much more than ritual, and the *pietas* of the Gascon gentleman was mechanized into official custom. "The soul," wrote Thomas Hobbes, " has no motions in itself." It became a popular view. But Hobbes had professed Christianity after a different style from Montaigne.

The ambiguous beliefs of Elizabeth of England, the ambiguous submission of Henry of Navarre—these and other things (including the strained relations between the Popes and the Kings, Catholic or other) had confused the Reformation. The Western half of Christendom settled into an uneasy division. But the division between the Roman Catholic and the Reformed Churches left both sides to suffer from the split within the " double man." Belief and disbelief became rather quantitative than qualitative. In England this was most noticeable in the conflict between orthodoxy and Deism. Deism is said first to have appeared in the writings of Lord Herbert of Cherbury, the brother of that brilliant young star, the Public Orator of Cambridge, Mr. George Herbert, who (in a sedate Anglican manner) renounced the world for God. And indeed there were plenty of his kind as well as his brother's about everywhere during all that changing epoch. Metaphysics took refuge in strange places, as for instance (to mention only England) in George Fox when he felt " the whole creation give forth a new smell to him " or when Mr. William Law, in a London bookseller's shop, was put into a dreadful sweat by casually opening a volume of Jacob Boehme, the Lutheran cobbler of High Germany whose close friends and disciples were two young Roman Catholic gentlemen, and whose disciple in England was the same Mr. Law. Mr. Law lived even more sedately than George Herbert; he lived, with two middle-aged ladies, in a manor in Northamptonshire at the beginning of the eighteenth century as Cowper lived with Mary Unwin at Olney towards the end. But the spiritual familiars of the one were the alchemical glories of Boehme, and of the other the horrid imps of a debased Calvinism. Law wrote in that retirement a few books which (allowing for a certain distrust of the reason provoked by the Deists and a certain ignorance of sensible communications, high though he rated matter) form perhaps one of the best statements of the pure Christian religion that have ever been issued. He defined in a sentence or two, in his *Christian Regeneration,* the great danger of the official Church : " when religion is in the hands of the mere natural man, he is always the worse for it; it adds a bad heat to his own dark fire and helps to inflame his four elements of selfishness, envy, pride, and wrath. . . . Their religion was according to the workings of their whole nature, and the old man was as busy and as much delighted in it as the new."

Deism, with its Pelagian man (soon to be turned into the Noble Savage—*plus ça change, plus c'est la même chose*), its judicious reason, its social morals, spread widely in England, and was with some difficulty argued down in the eighteenth century by the orthodox, who at one time entertained a hope that the Whig Government would suppress it by force. But the Government had other things to do;

it was, unintentionally, creating the British Empire, and was, intentionally, neglecting philosophy. The quality of disbelief had become a gentlemanly minimum of belief; and the eternal co-inherence of all mankind had been narrowed, at best, into the virtue of benevolence exercised according to the general understanding of the directions of " the absentee landlord " of the universe. The faintest lip-service of irony was still paid, by Hume and Gibbon, to the fainter image of Deity. But practically for the first time since the Roman Government had been troubled by the Church the secular government had ceased—except in the cases of political nuisances—to trouble about religion, or to persecute *proprio motu*.

On the Continent the state of affairs was not very different, though there were a few notable differences. Of these not the least was the existence, in the century after Montaigne, of one of the great Christian apologists. The " double man " of Montaigne provoked and stirred in Pascal a similar " double man." " It is not in Montaigne but in myself, that I find all that I see in him," but Pascal did not perhaps see all that there was in him, and he could not consent to the Gascon's ambiguity. He saw around him a society already cutting its fashionable coat in Montaigne's manner, but not wearing it at Mass with Montaigne's air. He revolted deeply against it. Something other than this easy reconciliation of man's double nature must be found, but he knew the double nature well enough : " We have an incapacity of proof, insurmountable by all dogmatism; we have an idea of truth, invincible to all scepticism." " All the principles of stoics, sceptics, atheists, etc., are true. But their conclusions are false, because the opposite principles are also true." " Our soul is cast into a body where it finds number, time, dimension. Thereupon it reasons, and calls this nature necessity, and can believe nothing else." This indeed, as one might say, " is talking." Reason is driven to call this communicated nature necessity, upon which necessity she erects her instruments. It is the old trouble which the wise Greek had seen so long ago : " Give

me an inch of earth to stand on and I will move the world."
But there is no inch of earth; there never has been; there
never—though " the heart has its reasons that the head does not
know "—can be. And so what?

The passionate propagandists of Christendom had never
before been in such a situation—or not, at least, since Constantine. Private conversations might have doubted, but
they had been really private conversations; whereas now the
conversations were becoming as public as the Rites at which
they delicately but deliberately shrugged. Never before since
Rome fell had it been so widely felt, so freely admitted, so
only half-formally denied, that there was nowhere an inch of
earth; in the France of the seventeenth century the acknow-
ledgment was only opening, but it was opening. The voice
of Bossuet, the piety of Fénelon, the devotion of Mme de
Maintenon and the old King Louis still rallied the ranks of
the believers. The Revocation in 1685 of the Edict of Nantes
which had granted toleration to the Huguenots was almost
the last gain of the older system, the last great dramatic
declaration that what a man believed was of importance.
The motto " *Que sçais-je?*" had indeed escaped from the
Gascon's library to run about the world. But the gay flutter-
ings of the society which welcomed it treated it as of little
more value than the *Credo* which it replaced. Morals fluttered
with them. The eyes of the austerer students of religion found
little to comfort them in the doctors and confessors of that
society. These were largely drawn from that other society of
Jesus, and they desired (or so it seemed) no more of an
inch of moral earth than of metaphysical. The science of
casuistry ruled all, and to the precisians casuistry looked, like
the Indulgences of an earlier day, very much as if it were a
" permission to sin." " Probabilism " had come in : the doctrine that if you were in doubt about the moral propriety of
an act, and if you found a reasonable weight of opinion in
favour of it among the casuists, that was good enough; even
if an equal—some said, even if a greater—weight of opinion
were against it. It does not seem a very perilous doctrine,

except that it allowed for two opinions upon the details of right and wrong—a thing abhorrent to devout " Puritan " minds. The Dutchman Jansen and his followers saw and trembled; they invoked truth; they invoked sanctity; they invoked—inevitable and fatal error!—Augustine. The usual controversy broke out, and was settled at last in the usual manner; the Jansenist movement was crushed. Not even the royal effort to establish a Gallican Church in more or less independence of Rome saved them. One claim of their rigid purity will serve for an example : they declared that Grace did not exist outside the Church. But this was denied by the highest authorities in the Church.

Pascal was a friend and intimate of Jansenists. He was a mathematician, and knew the doctrines of chances and of infinity. He had known the workings of something like mystical experience. He turned all three elements in his nature on to a plan to convert the world around him; he proposed to write an Apology for the whole thing; he began to make notes for the volume. He proposed to controvert Montaigne; say rather, " subvert." He could undercut and undermine the *Essays.* He put down his jottings, the *Thoughts.* He disliked Montaigne's levity as much as his thought. He demanded that all men should *choose.* Mathematician that he was, he knew infinity; Jansenist that he was, he felt the dangers of infinity—felt and feared them for others. " The finite to stake . . . the infinite to gain." Could anyone consent to doubt? He conceded his imagined opponent a feeble if intelligent murmur : " The true course is not to wager at all," and crushed himself with the awful answer : " Yes, but you *must* wager. It is not optional."

He was, of course, right; it is no more optional than death. He was right; in the last analysis Christendom must choose belief and not any quality of belief, however fine. It is the more necessary therefore whenever possible to colour belief with the finest qualities, and not only with itself; the divine co-inherence allows and encourages all the shooting lights of human wisdom, human folly, human courtesy.

Pascal, like all believers, was a public danger. But he was a danger of that kind by virtue of which only Christendom has managed to exist at all.

Something of the same sort was true of his famous *Provincial Letters*. He attacked the casuistry of the Jesuits with, it seems, some justification. But there again he put everything on one throw. As he said to Montaigne: "No; you must wager; abandon ambiguity; believe—and only believe," so he said, if not to the Jesuits at least to their penitents: "No, you must wager; abandon casuistry; be completely pure—and only pure." It is wholly admirable; only—he gibed at the Fathers of the Society for having said that a servant did not sin if he made his wages up to the market-value of his services by stealing from his master. It is indeed a scandalous doctrine; it seems to permit theft. Only by chance does it occur to one that Pascal is coming near to damning, on his own showing, any underpaid servant-girl who pockets a penny her mistress has left about. Perhaps he did not intend it, but here at least one can follow him to a single rule: if the servant-girl is excusable, then the Jesuits were technically right; if Pascal is right, then she is (except by repentance) damned. The Apostolic Church, by and large, and despite the saints, has always known better.

Pascal died; Jansenism was denounced; the Gallican movement broke down. But the steady movement of retrogression went on everywhere. The Society of Jesus was accused of this and the other; it was denounced as immoral by an immoral society; and what Pascal had supposed to be inexcusable was repudiated by those who treated Pascal only as a master of French prose. M. de Saint-Simon, that marvel of malice, worldliness, and cleverness, wrote his *Memoirs*. Frederick—afterwards the Great—ascended the Throne of Prussia, and annexed all the Enlightenment he could get. He established a Throne, which, alone of all in Europe, made no pretence to depend upon the Grace of God. Everywhere society became more and more enlightened. By which was largely meant that whereas in the Middle Ages the questions that could not be answered theologically were held as negligible, in this century the answers that could not be given scientifically were more and more held to be worthless.

Intellectual enlightenment is apt to leave morals—especially public morals—where they were. The heavy mass of the ruling classes might be, within, witty and cultured, but on those without it lay with a heavy weight of self-indulged cruelty, luxury, and tyranny. "Wit, good verse, sincere enthusiasm, a lucid exposition of whatever in the human mind perpetually rebels against transcendental affirmations, were allowed every latitude and provoked no effective reply. But overt acts of disrespect to ecclesiastical authority were punished with rigour."[5] A dim horror begins to cover the ruling classes of Europe, a horror to which the later industrialists were heirs. The horror is of a body powerful, stupid, conservative, and cruel. In the eighteenth century the most famous man in all Europe found a name for it; he cried in a voice we cannot and must not forget: "*Ecrasez l'Infame*": "destroy the Infamy."

He did not altogether mean the Church alone by that, or if so, he meant the Church precisely when it had become an evil parody of itself. He was, however we take it, the first pure antagonist; he attacked the Church—and not in the name of Christ. He struck his blows so that the very memory of them has recalled her to her better self—that is, to the Holy Ghost. For thirteen hundred years she had not been in a position to be attacked from outside; there had, in fact, been no outside. She had been denounced only by her members, even if they were heretical members, except where the alien cymbals of Islam had challenged her. But the clash of these new cymbals refused membership—in favour of a God not so unlike the God of Islam. Intellectually the cymbals were a little brassy. Voltaire seems actually to have thought on a low level; he did suppose that the fact that

[5] *The French Revolution*, Hilaire Belloc.

there were a thousand reputed Saviours of the world proved that there was no Saviour of the world, and that the different circumstances and natures of many mothers of many gods disproved the Virginity of the Mother of God. We know that neither affirmation nor denial are as simple as that. But in matters of public morals Voltaire shocked and justly shook the Church. The mechanical operation of cruelty which proceeded under the automatic rigour of the still officially Christian governments was halted, for a few brief moments, by the incredible energy of the old man at Ferney. The Calas case at Toulouse had been an exhibition of offensive and habitual—how habitual!—bestiality. That a Huguenot family had suffered at the hands of a Catholic magistracy was an accident of the country; in France things had that particular colour. The important thing was that an ordinary family had suffered under the solemn manias of officialdom— and unjustly even by officialdom's own regulations. In this and in other cases Voltaire attacked in force and with a passion of sincerity : " I will not laugh while such things are done." He wrote across the brain of all future Christendom : *" Ecrasez l'Infame."* Christendom will be unwise if ever she forgets that cry, for she will have lost touch with contrition once more. She had forgotten—or at least her rulers had forgotten—Man; the candles burned to the incarnate, but the co-inherence of all men was being lost. It was supposed outside her that Christendom was changing, that the Catholic Church was dead, and that the name of Christ was soon to be as forgotten as that of any of the dukes of Edom or the princes of Gomorrah.

The claims and cries of men were left to those of the Enlightened who were willing to listen—as Voltaire was. When on his last visit to Paris he was received with a fury of triumph by all classes, the Academicians praised him for his writing and the sceptics for his wit. But it is said that in the roaring crowd outside the theatre, as he was got to his carriage, someone said to a woman : " Who is it?" and she answered in her passion : " It is Voltaire who has saved the family of Calas." When he died, he was buried, by hasty arrangements, in consecrated ground; there was certainly no reason why he should be, and the priest responsible suffered. The ecclesiastical authorities would have preferred him to be tossed dead in a ditch, since he could not, alive, be broken like Calas on the wheel. During the Revolution his body was brought to the Pantheon in procession, with the writing : " He made us ready to be free." The myth of supernatural justice and the fact of earthly justice were, in that age, too much opposed, and their reconciliation yet delays.

There was, nevertheless, beyond the realms of the Enlightenment, and touched by it in its monarchical society only to a limited extent, a new organization of the Idea. In the year 1472 the Grand Prince of Moscow had married Zoe, the niece of the last Emperor of the East, who had been brought up in Rome. The Prince had added the eagle with two heads to his arms, to signify that he was the heir to Byzantium, and in fact he so far carried on the tradition that in his lifetime the Mongol domination over Muscovy was lost. But it was not till a century later in 1591 that a new Patriarchate was established by the general consent of the Patriarchs of Constantinople, Alexandria, Antioch, and Jerusalem. The myth of the City was maintained; it was solemnly professed that Moscow was the Third Rome, and from another centre the Orthodoxy of the East denounced the heretical schism of Old Rome and the Popes. But the high tradition was not allowed to last in that form. In the eighteenth century another city rose on the Baltic, and another Peter established there the most effective power of the Orthodox. The theology of the Golden Horn appeared on the banks of the Neva. The Tsar abolished the Patriarchate and substituted the Holy Governing Synod. But also he established all that we mean by Russia, and over the thousands of miles of that new Empire the peasants settled to the peace of the half-priestly monarch. Nevertheless the sacerdotalism of the Emperor was rather a splendour than an activity; there also the Head was Christ.

In the year 1773 the Orthodox Tsarina of Russia, the Catholic Emperor of Austria, and the . . . the King of Prussia finally partitioned Poland. It was the great political exhibition of the Enlightenment.

CHAPTER IX

THE RETURN OF THE MANHOOD

Voltaire had denounced the Infamy. But not Voltaire, nor
a France of Voltaires, could do more than shake and anger
the Infamy. They could not destroy or redeem it. For that
something else was required, some movement more within
Christendom than ever Voltaire could be, however he derived
from Christendom, some stir in the mass of Christendom.
That mass remained—the innumerable honest priests and
pious laity labouring, " all and every of these in their several
calling," to the glory of God and the service of the Co-
inherence. Mutually guilty, mutually redeemed, they toiled
and adored—stupid perhaps, but patient and believing, from
the Russian peasant beyond Nijni-Novgorod to the servant-
girl in a Scottish presbytery. Even among that mass the tide of
Christendom was receding. In its " last and lowest ebb "
it sank away into the solitary and devoted lives which were,
are, and always must be, the fountains of her deeps; her
spectacles and her geniuses are marvellous, but her unknown
saints are her power.

Even while Voltaire, in the name of Humanity, fought for
men, two of the geniuses began to unloose the fountains and
call out the power. In England John Wesley, in South Italy
Alphonsus Liguori, pronounced with passion to the lowest
classes of that eighteenth-century world the Name of Salvation. Had they ever met—say on the deck of some small
sailing-ship in Lisbon Harbour—they would not have approved
of each other. Yet they had a thing in common—at least some
of the common people heard them gladly. Wesley against
his will (the will of a High Church Anglican of Oxford)
was to found one of the greatest of the Free Churches, one
of the last and sincerest efforts to base religion on actual

experience and not on formal belief. Alphonsus, against *his* will (so certain is sanctity), was to be canonized with peculiar honours by Pope Pius VII and declared a doctor of the Roman Church by Pius IX. It was certainly he who, of the two, exercised the greater influence on Christendom through his papal admirers, and the promulgation of the doctrines of the Immaculate Conception and the Infallibility derive partly from him. He was instrumental also in establishing, though he did not originate, the devotions to " the sacred human Heart of Jesus " and to the Heart of Mary. There is about such devotions a peculiar subtlety of intention and of idea which this is not the place to discuss. It seems that there had been in the seventeenth century a devotion " to the Heart of Jesus and Mary." " The extraordinary use of the singular rather than the plural suggests that *heart* was regarded primarily as a metaphorical word for love."[1] The violence of some of the pictorial representations of the Sacred Heart is not to blind us to the fact that it was in fact the human Heart of Messias, the love between himself and his mortal Mother, which was markedly to beat both in the Church and the world during the next century, when the blood of men pulsated more passionately in their own veins.[2]

Wesley would have cared little for the Devotion of the Sacred Heart, and even less for the moral Probabilism of St. Alphonsus. Even Newman hesitated; but then Newman all his life retained something of the English gentleman. His notorious quarrel with Kingsley was on that score, and he won it because Kingsley was less of a writer and even more of a gentleman. But Wesley stirred the Evangelicals of his own land, and the result was that while Liguori began to affect, as it were, the capital of Christendom, so those renewed souls in England began to affect its provinces. The world

---

[1] *Religion since the Reformation,* Leighton Pullan.

[2] It has been said that in Latin Christendom " the line of Augustinian influence continues to sink until it reaches its nadir at the canonization of Alfonso Liguori " (*The Ideas of the Fall,* Dr. N. P. Williams.) The sentence illuminates the history of the nineteenth century.

of Voltaire, of Frederick of Prussia, of Leopold of Austria ("my brother the sacristan," as Frederick called him), was entirely ignorant of what was happening. The Deists were still arguing and the altar candles were burning. The *Theos* of the Divine Ambiguity was formally, if dubiously, adored. But the Spirit did not allow the *anthropos* to be neglected. Within and without the Church He allowed humanity to return.

In England, apart from the Methodist conversions, the revolution began at the ends of the earth. It has not been within the scope of this book to describe the missionary efforts of the Church beyond Europe. The Church in China, in India, in Africa, in the further West, has not hitherto deeply affected the central ideas and movement of Christendom; that may very well be to happen in the future. But a false limitation is set up if one does not realize that the energy of Christendom had been, through all those centuries, pushing itself continually abroad. In the earlier centuries some of the views denounced by authority in the West had spread eastward, as, for example, the Nestorian heresy. "A chain of (Nestorian) bishops and churches spread from Jerusalem to Pekin."[8] They had by no means failed when the first Franciscans and Dominicans appeared there in the thirteenth and fourteenth century, and the legend of Prester John reflects the dim European knowledge of the Christendom on the other side of the world. In India the same testifying, even if mistaken, body was found by Portuguese missions in the sixteenth century, and by the end of the century was re-integrated into the Roman Church. The court of the Khalif of Islam was recurrently attacked, by St. Francis, by Raymond Lull a little later, and (in 1658) by Mary Fisher, a sedate and ardent Quaker from Yorkshire. The coming of the Jesuits brought a new army to the support of doctrine and charity without as well as within Europe. Francis Xavier appeared in Japan and within fifty years there were hundreds of thousands of Christians, who were eventually destroyed by persecution. In the West the activity of the Jesuits is one

[8] *Missions,* Louise Creighton.

of the more famous histories of the world; they reciprocated in word and action what had been always the purpose of Christendom—defence of natural human rights, assertion of free supernatural grace, the peculiar relation of every soul—Indian as much as European—to Almighty God. It was, some fifty years ago, the fashion in England to denigrate the Jesuits and their missions; it is now become more fashionable to denigrate the missions of the Reformed Churches, and in fact they were a little late. But they came; and while the Jesuits were suffering at the hands of the Indians in tortures such as even Europe had hardly rivalled, John Eliot was teaching and translating among the tribes. From Rome the Congregation of Propaganda directed everywhere their great assault; from the Protestant countries the various societies raided the continents and seas. The nature of man as well as the Name of God was declared to the whole world.

As in Europe, however, so abroad. The creed of Christ and the greed of men ran side by side. In spite of all protests and all denunciations slavery, which had slowly disappeared from Europe, was re-established by Europe in the further lands, and showed signs of returning to Europe. The Protestant Churches and the Roman Church alike made conveniences for it, the Protestants informally, the Romans more formally.[4] It may be conceded that slavery is not, formally, anti-Christian, so long as the slave's natural and supernatural rights are preserved. But the proper preservation of those rights is apt to make nonsense of slavery.

It has always seemed impossible to prevent the English becoming more moral about distresses in Lagos than about distresses in London, and so it was at the end of the eighteenth century. William Wilberforce, the protagonist of the reform, showed no signs of knowing the horrible evils at home. He never seemed to be acutely aware of the sufferings of children in cotton mills, though he did certainly agree that

---

[4] " A papal bull (1537) sanctioned the opening of a slave market in Lisbon, where ten to twelve thousand negroes were sold annually for transportation to the West Indies." *Missions,* Louise Creighton.

children of twelve ought not to work more than eleven hours a day. He helped to found the Church Missionary Society and also the Society for the Suppression of Vice, and he had no idea of allowing mental liberty to the English poor. Still in fact, however much pity and justice he lacked, he and his friends did fight for the pity and justice they understood. They left too much of horror alone, but they did interfere with horror; pain was a little less prevalent when they had finished. Sincerely or insincerely they did maintain that barbarians must not be made slaves. And they did it with a conviction that this was their Christian duty.

Wilberforce himself had passed through a period of worldliness—he went to the theatre, dined with the Prime Minister, and enjoyed society. But he was taken by heart-searchings, " a strong conviction of my guilt,"[5] and by misery. He was recovered (by a coincidence, one would think, of the Holy Ghost) from this state by the Reverend John Newton, once a slave-trader, then an Evangelical clergyman, Rector of St. Mary Woolnoth, and a friend of Cowper's. Whatever effect Newton had had upon Cowper, his effect on Wilberforce was wholly good; he brought him out into " serenity, tranquillity, composure which is not to be destroyed." And it seems probable that it was by Newton he must have been encouraged to his mission, or at least that it was from Newton that he learnt enough to turn him to his mission. He had had predecessors—Roman, Anglican, Dissenting. The American Colonies had protested against the Slave Trade. Lord Mansfield in 1772 had laid it down that the power to own slaves " never was in use here or acknowledged by the law." On 12 May, 1789 Wilberforce in the House of Commons moved twelve resolutions for the suppression of the Slave Trade. The high humanitarian gentlemen of the eighteenth century drew up behind him, when " by divine grace " (as he wrote in his diary) he made his motions. " The House, the nation, and Europe, are under great and serious obliga-

[5] *Wilberforce*, R. Coupland; from which the other quotations are taken.

tions to the honourable gentleman," said Burke. Pitt, on a later night, closed an all-night debate by quoting Latin verses of liberty and hope under the growing sunlight in the House. " Go on," the dying Wesley wrote to Wilberforce, " in the name of God and the power of his might." But the opposition was strong. The Earl of Westmoreland, like a less reputable pagan of the second century, declared : " Though I should see the Presbyterian and the prelate, the methodist and the field-preacher, the Jacobin and the murderer, unite in support of it [the motion against the Trade], yet in this House I will raise my voice against it." Indeed he foresaw something not far from the truth; a movement not unlike the union of the prelate, the Methodist, and the Jacobin was to distinguish the next century. On 25 March (the Feast of the Annunciation) in 1807 the Abolitionist Bill was passed : " all manner of dealing and trading " in slaves was " utterly abolished, prohibited, and declared to be unlawful." The result was referred by Wilberforce to the " goodness and glory " of Almighty God. He pressed on to abolish it universally. He urged on Castlereagh; he was received by the Tsar Alexander. At last he succeeded; Europe forbade the Trade. He succeeded further; he destroyed the institution. On 31 July, 1834, eight hundred thousand slaves were, by the process of British law, declared free.

Meanwhile in France the mass itself had moved; the Revolution had come, and all Europe was altered. On 17 June 1789, a month after Wilberforce had moved his resolutions, the Commons of France, the third House of the States-General, joined by a few of the clergy, declared themselves the National Assembly of France and swore not to separate without giving the nation a Constitution. The history of the Revolution is no part of the present business. What is remarkable is that, just as it was Christendom which had led the attack on the Slave Trade and defeated it, at a time when it was supposed that Christendom was all but dead, so in France, at a time of the same hypothesis, it was found that Christendom was already reviving. The Revolution in 1790 decreed the

Civil Constitution of the Clergy; it was denounced by the Roman See. The prim genius of Robespierre devoted the militant crowds of Paris and the provinces to the Goddess of Reason, and the sky-blue coat he wore on the occasion flashes before us like the last gleam of a Deistic and rational heaven. The massacres of the priests showed the darker colour of Christian martyrdom.

In the last fifty years of the eighteenth century the Church had faded; in the first fifty years of the nineteenth it returned everywhere with astonishing vitality; and it returned not as morals or as humanitarianism, but as doctrine. Doctrine might or might not lead to humanitarianism, to social revolution, and it more and more tended to do so; but within the Church those things came from strengthening and not from weakening doctrine. The power of dogma returned and, on the whole, returned without individual leaders. Such leaders there were, but if they were lost the movement did not cease. There were no Calvins or Dominics or Augustines. The man who was most like those great ones was a Dane, a contemporary of Hans Andersen, but though Hans Andersen achieved world-wide repute at once, Sören Kierkegaard had to wait for his through some seventy years. It has taken Christendom that long to catch him up; it took it fifty to catch up St. Thomas, and it has not caught up Dante yet. He coordinated experiences in a new manner; say, using the old word, that he caused alien and opposite experiences to coinhere. He was the type of the new state of things in which Christendom had to exist, and of the new mind with which Christendom knew them. He lived under a sense of judgment, of contrition, of asceticism; but also (and equally) of revolt, of refusal, of unbelief. Almost always before his days one of these two things had triumphed over the other; or if not, if there had been others like him, then their words had been so lightly read that it was supposed that one had triumphed. No doubt, as soon as Kierkegaard becomes fashionable, which is already beginning to happen, that fate will fall upon him. He will be explained; the other half of him (whichever that may be) will be excused. His imagination will be made to depend on his personal history, and his sayings will be so moderated in our minds that they will soon become not his sayings but ours. It is a very terrible thing to consider how often this has happened with the great, and how often we are contented to understand what we have neatly supposed that they have said. " There is," wrote Kierkegaard, " no temple-robber, toiling in shackles of iron, so vicious as those who pillage among sacred things; and even Judas, who sold his Master for thirty pieces of silver, is not more despicable than those who traffic in great deeds." That we traffic from good motives, to ease a friend or soothe a death-bed or encourage a conscience, does not alter the despicable fact of the traffic.

He forbade us resignation; he denied tragedy; he was a realist and unbeliever—both in this world and in the other; and his life of scepticism was rooted in God. " God is that which demands absolute love." His father, as a boy, had stood in the dunes of Jutland and cursed God, but it is false to explain and excuse him by that, for his other-worldliness has accepted that, and his reconciliation is from beyond it. In that he is like Adam. His imagination is born of his father's act, and has brought his father's act back into the economy of fear and trembling and of the divine Salvation. In that he is like St. John. He has turned Catholics into agnostics, for they have not been able to bear that synthesis of reconciliation which cannot be defined except in his own books. He has turned agnostics into Catholics, for they have felt in him an answer of the same kind as the question, an answer as great as the question. Most Christian answers to agnosticism seem not to begin to understand the agnosticism; they seem to invoke the compassion of God. In Kierkegaard one feels that God does not understand that kind of compassion.

It was in 1853, in the last year of his life, that he opened an attack upon the Danish Church. He attacked it because it was the Church of his country, the Church he knew, not because it was less Christian or more guilty than others, for to his mind all the instituted Churches were guilty—so guilty as to be unaware of their guilt. The attack, though he did not perhaps fully realize it, was in the best tradition of Christendom; it blew the old prophetic trumpet. It was, in fact, part of the revival of Christendom; it was the cry of, the demand for, contrition *now*, always now. An old and venerable leader of the Church, Bishop Mynster, had died; he had been called in the funeral sermon " a witness to the truth." Kierkegaard attacked : "Was Mynster a witness to the truth?" The answer was probably yes, but that Mynster himself thought so, and the more the hierarchy (except under persecution) think they are witnessing to the truth, the more official, the more untrue, becomes their witness to that certitude.

But Kierkegaard was not alone in his attack. All over Europe some kind of shrill call of doctrine and of dogma was rising. An awareness was springing up, sometimes in one form, sometimes in another. In England the Oxford Movement was already in action; Newman's Tract 90 had appeared in 1840, and Newman himself was received into the Roman Church in 1848. It was supposed he would be followed by his followers, but they were not his followers as much as they were followers of religion, and religion did not lead them with him. Neither of those two great schismatics, Wesley nor Newman, shook the centre of the Church of England, nor could; what they did was to direct attention to some sin, some negligence, some chill. Fervour awoke again, and doctrine, or perhaps not so much doctrine as the assertion of doctrine. And as in England, so elsewhere. In 1840 there was a dispute over marriage-laws in Prussia; bishops were imprisoned, and again Christendom awoke to a militant consciousness. In France Lamennais and Montalembert called the Roman Church to come to the aid of the Revolution and the poor; they desired to separate the Church from its bourgeois friends, and when Lamennais' theories were refused he abandoned the Church. But, like the rest, he remained acutely aware of it, and Christendom remained aware of the poor.

The Way of the Affirmation of Images had returned. Kierkegaard perhaps, of them all, most resembled the other, the Negative Way. "God is that which demands absolute love." But he did not deny the Affirmations any more than the rest of them denied the Negation. The whole period was in fact, full of the combination of those two great Ways. The Negation grew alive with difference; the Affirmation maintained doctrine and charity. In 1854 Pius IX, as if in a most proper image of both, decreed of his own authority to all the world the dogma of the Immaculate Conception of the *anthropotokos,* of the Virgin-Mother of the Deivirilis. Christendom was not agreed on it; neither the Eastern Churches nor the Protestant Churches approved, nor perhaps understood. But certainly the Manhood had returned; within and without Christendom the millions stirred, and Karl Marx wrote of a classless society on earth.

The enemy in those years was supposed to be not so much Karl Marx, of whom few had heard, as Liberalism. The number of meanings which the word may have in English has made it difficult to use simply. For generally those who have wanted liberty have not apprehended dogma, and those who have apprehended dogma have not wanted liberty. Liberalism in religion and liberalism in politics are not the same thing, however often they are confused, by the friends and the enemies of either. But the spread of doctrine had been accompanied, both within and without the Church, by the spread of that other desire which may roughly be described by the word Liberty. It would not be true to say that Liberty as an idea had not been considered in itself since the early Roman Empire, but it would not be so very untrue. All through the Middle Ages and through the Reformation Augustine's phrase that liberty comes by grace and not grace by liberty had been at the bottom of the organization and imposition of belief. To be properly free man must be in a state of salvation, and there had been through those centuries less enthusiasm for the idea of his being improperly free—free in a merely temporal sense. It was approved, it was even encouraged, but it was conditioned by the very much more important necessity of offering him the supernatural freedom. What mattered was not that he should be able to speculate as he chose but that he should be able to act as he chose. Only the service of God supplied that perfect freedom, and men, as far as possible, were to be compelled to come in to that service. Messias and his Apostles had not spent a great deal of time talking about freedom and personal independence and individualism and a man's right to his own opinions. Nor, when the quality of disbelief was rediscovered and the upper classes went all Deist or infidel, was that freedom supposed to relate to the lower classes. Lord Chesterfield did not think one ought to discuss religion before the servants, any more than he thought his servants ought to help govern the country. But what with one thing and another, the idea that everyone ought to be as free as possible had spread widely during the nineteenth century. Even then (and even now) that farther development of liberty which has been nobly defined to be " the protection and not the persecution of the Opposition "[6] had not spread far. It was not easy for it to spread in Christendom, for, by definition, Christendom cannot fundamentally admit the right of an Opposition (to its dogmas) to exist; to refuse the Co-inherence is to separate oneself from the nature of things. Add to that abstract difficulty the more concrete difficulty of any hierarchy refraining from interference with things beyond its scope, and the tendency of the friends of freedom to deny that dogma can ever be justified, and the quarrel between the claims of liberty and the claims of grace was well set, quite apart from those distracting new ideas of science and of scholarship which were to encourage it.

In 1850 Kierkegaard had defined, from his own particular point of view, the movement of the world about him. He had already mocked at the easy kind of modern " doubt " which he

[6] *The Times,* 7 January, 1939.

saw, in that world, praised and admired. It was not the doubt
which Pascal had combated and Montaigne had encouraged;
it was something of which men were proud, and therefore
it was not real experience, for it is impossible to be proud
of experience : that happens. One can never be anything
but humble about that. So that it seemed to him, that the
opposition to Christianity was as futile as was much of contemporary Christianity. He saw it—he saw his own times—
as an effort to be without "the unconditional." "Let the
race, let each individual, make the experiment of doing without the unconditional—it is a whirlpool and remains such.
In the meanwhile, for a longer or shorter period, it may
seem otherwise, it may seem like stability and security. But
at bottom, it is and remains a whirlpool. . . . To live in the
unconditional, inhaling only the unconditional, is impossible
to man; he perishes, like the fish forced to live in the air.
But on the other hand, without relating himself to the unconditional, man cannot, in the deepest sense, be said to
'live.'" In fact, of course, the better opposition did not see
itself so; rather, like Lucretius, it conceived itself to be
freeing mankind from a condition which hampered its
proper movement, and which it had supposed was on the
point of expiring. It seems likely that that great effort
of the Middle Ages towards the imposition of belief had
printed itself so deeply on the mind of Europe that, wherever
the Church still lived and moved, it was regarded (however
falsely) as still dominant. But also the Church both demanded and promised not the liberty of time and place but
the unconditional liberty of the co-inherent Kingdom which
was precisely free from time and place. But if she does not
promise the lesser liberty she does not reject it; it is a
matter of comparative indifference to her.

"Never," Kierkegaard had written, "have 'opinions' (the
most heterogeneous, in the most various fields) felt themselves
under 'Liberty, Equality, Fraternity,' so free, so unhampered,
so fortunate, with the rules of go as you please which is expressed in the motto 'up to a certain point.'" "The liberty of

each limited by the like liberty of all," wrote John Stuart Mill, and defined, in that relation, "the certain point." Liberty meant to have a right to have your own opinions, to propagate your own opinions, and to behave according to your own opinions—subject to a similar freedom inherent in each member of the community, and the whole organized by the whole community, or as much of the community as possible. Reviving and militant Christendom denied the "right" to hold false opinions. Unfortunately a dying and stagnant Christendom was always saying the same thing. That the heart of the Church, feeling (to quote Kierkegaard again) that "before God man is always in the wrong," should abandon all claims and all rights was not surprising. But the alternative phrase, that "before God man is always justifiable," which was alien to the working Church, was a kind of watchword of the opposition, and its rejection by a vocal hierarchy was quite different from its rejection by the working Church. Unfortunately the Church is not the hierarchy; much less any odd member of the hierarchy. The Church knew (in spite of Lorenzo Valla) all of importance that there was to know, and what it did not know—if not exactly "not knowledge"—was unimportant to man in his present condition. But on the other hand the populace of Christendom (the mental populace) were apt to be shocked and horrified at any change in that (by definition) unimportant knowledge. The great scientific discoveries of that age (or what then purported to be scientific discoveries) threw both Christendom and non-Christendom very much out of control. The pious feared that they might, and the impious thought they undoubtedly had, upset Christendom. This was excusable in the impious, but inexcusable in the pious. The pious, however, then as always, were in a state of high anxiety to defend and protect, and generally stand up for, Almighty God. The expansion of time and space caused both the scientific and religious leaders to talk as if the Omnipotence could not possibly devote as much attention to a minor star as to a central—as if that which underlies all proportion was bound to be dominated by size. There still faintly lingers in places the image of the Godhead abandoning the earth to its own affairs because it is "such a little one." And in those days the dispute was much more vivid. But "the unconditional" was not, in fact, involved.

The great advance of scholarship was more acceptable. The many new opportunities offered it, the fact that (for practically the first time) scholarship was free to pronounce its own judgment on certain complicated points, the intense moral integrity involved both for orthodox and unorthodox scholars, the infinite multiplication of what one might call "the conditional" in all that research, all this gave to the new schools, of whatever colour, a true and honourable value. Biblical criticism, history, archæology, anthropology, all revelled in the gladsome light; the light of the mind that read hieroglyphics, the light of the sun that shone again on houses, fortifications, streets and temples buried for two or three thousand years. The humanitarian Jesus appeared, with the fearful and fiend-like face of St. Paul looking over his shoulder, and hypnotizing the simple credulity of the early Church into accepting Oriental mysteries. Presently indeed there was nothing left but St. Paul, for the historic Jesus vanished altogether, and St. John was resolved into Plato. Yet the one thing that grew more and more certain on all sides was that the Church had begun in the midst of rites and dogmas. The fair and faint dream of a simple Gospel became more and more of a dream.

On the other hand the attack on miracles took on a new energy. Lecky and Huxley, in England, defined with the most admirably lucid moderation their case against miracles and made it clear that the only *final* case against miracles was the dogma that they did not happen. So it became clear also that the only *final* case against Incarnation was the dogma that the Nature of God could not or would not incarnate. All else was evidence, dispute, judgment. The great arguments continued, and continue to-day; it is much to be hoped that they will not stop. Never before had the serious critical and historical arguments against Christianity had a chance to be properly put forward; never before had they had a chance to be—not answered, for what arguments of the kind can ever be answered? but—understood and enjoyed. Scholarship opened on all sides, and all sides discovered its limitations.

For all sides took advantage of it. Doctrine advanced on the lines of scholarship as well as its opponents. Learning assisted and developed belief. Respectable English clergymen went to prison—possibly a not too uncomfortable prison, but still prison—for technical points of theology and ritual. The Judicial Committee of the Privy Council fought a losing battle against ideas which had been, in the Church of England, not so much forgotten as comatose. Nor was learning left to fight alone. The Bible Christians and the Plymouth Brethren sprang into being. The Wesleyan body split and re-split, and each body multiplied its members; and from one of the smaller of those bodies emerged the figure of William Booth, General in the Army of Salvation, and the drums and the red flags went into horrible places, and men were set on and knocked about for their testimony, but the Precious Blood beat in the march of the Army towards God, while in France It had fructified in the silence and sweetness of the Curé d'Ars, and at Lourdes the waters sprang for healing under the direction of the *Anthropotokos,* and everywhere also the practice of more frequent communion began to return; the age of confirmation began to be lowered; the mystical Oblation urged itself upon all.

But the greatest union of the claims of learning and of the supernatural was not in England nor in France—nor even in Germany where priests were imprisoned (more seriously than in England), and even certain members of the hierarchy, in the struggle called the *Kulturkampf.* The most spectacular, and incomparably the most important, declaration of doctrine took place at Rome when, on 18 June, 1870, amid the most famous thunderstorm in all history, the Infallibility of the Roman Pontiff was decreed in the Basilica of St. Peter, and the declaration of the Council of Vatican re-asserted the supernatural scheme of all things. Voltaire had not been dead a hundred years, and everywhere " the unconditional " was again a common thought—like it or not, believe it or not.

The close of the nineteenth century therefore saw the position of Christendom in Europe much like it had been after the conversion of Constantine. There was the mass of doctrinally active Christendom, and there was the other mass of opposition, also based fundamentally on dogma. There were, however, two great differences. The first was that, on the whole, the movement of the intellectual fashion of the day had set against Christendom, as in that earlier period it had set for Christendom. Social importance, in 1870 and onwards, remained for a little on the Christian side, as it had done in the eighteenth century. The middle-class in England, for example, did not wholly lose the habit of going to church until they acquired motor-cars (so negligible in the end is intellect itself). But science and scholarship were already accidentally providing them with colloquial conveniences for its rejection. The " conditional " (soon to be widely and warmly welcomed as Relativity—the popular, not the scientific, Relativity) was acquired even more easily than the motor-car. Such a great work as the *Golden Bough,* for example, was too easily supposed to have proved what it had never meant—or should never have meant—to prove. Its hinted thesis that all religion arose from a desire to encourage the annual harvest was generally thought to have explained satisfactorily how the harvest came into existence at all, and its multitudes of gods conditioned by magic were identified with a Godhead unconditioned except by Its own Will. In the perpetual struggle about the old question of which came first—the hen or the egg, the hen-fanciers had developed new schools and new energy. But the egg became more and more the social favourite, and the incubationists rashly supposed themselves, in the words of a leading French atheist, to have put out in heaven the lights that no man should relume.

But the second difference between that period and the years of Constantine was of very much greater importance. The movement of the dispossessed had proceeded all through the century. The consciousness of the primal physical needs of the oppressed multitudes spread and became militant. In the thirteenth century the presence of the Sacred Body and Blood had been formally defined to exist in the Eucharist. But now, both without and within Christendom, the natural body and blood of common men asserted their rights. Within Christendom this certainly had been implicit from the beginning—implicit in the life and acts of Messias, implicit in the belief that matter was capable of salvation, implicit in that insistence on Justice which had been declared almost as much as it had been neglected. It had been often enough explicit, in the Apocalypse, in many medieval sermons, in the definitions of the schoolmen, in the orations of Latimer and Bossuet, in the sympathy of many priests with the Revolution, in the labours of Wilberforce and Shaftesbury. It could never be the chief concern of Christendom; that must always be the " substance " as against the " sensuality "—to use the Lady Julian's words. But neither the Lady Julian nor the Church ever separated the two. " Both for the body and the soul," said the Rituals; and the Lady Julian : " In the self point that our Soul is made sensual, in the self point is the City of God ordained to him from without beginning." The communicated Eucharist held the double co-inherence. Natural justice was a necessary preliminary to all charity. This, which had always been a principle, stirred like other doctrine in the nineteenth century—especially, but not only, in the Christendom of America. But it stirred even more violently outside Christendom.

The many problems of social justice tended to concentrate on one—the question of property. Is there in man a natural and inalienable right to own? Christendom had asserted that there was; those who had rejected the principle had in the past been dealt with as heretics, and those who had refused property had generally been professed as Religious. Nor would Christendom now deny that decision. But it was true also that never before the nineteenth century had there been so much property to be owned or (proportionately) so few allowed to own it. Millions instead of thousands were dispossessed, and wholly dispossessed. The Roman people had of old been appeased with bread and circuses. But in this later age both had vanished. The poor were allowed neither corn nor carnival. Magnificence had ceased to be a virtue, and meals had ceased to be supplied. Mere hunger pre-occupied the lowest classes, and insecurity crept more and more among the lives of the middle-classes. The lower ranks of the bourgeois slipped steadily into the abyss; the higher crowded and clung together and desperately fought among themselves.

Christendom was largely identified by the revolutionaries with the owners of property, as well as with the abstract defence of property. This view was not so incorrect as it ought to have been. The theologians might accurately define, and the saints might labour on behalf of the poor, but all this was hampered by three things. The first was the un-doubted fact that the co-inherence of sensuality in substance, however true, however just, was of no great interest to those whose sensuality was only a continual despair. An anguish of need and more need can only be used as the Way by those already advanced in sanctity; the authorities of the Church were never intended to impose (or even too much to seem to impose) such a terrible Rejection of Images upon their co-inheritors of glory. No doubt there were some few who followed that Way even so, but of those to whom it was a mockery and an obscene parody of grace there were millions. The second difficulty was that the mass of professing Christians were definitely not in want of food, nor did they show any signs of selling much of what they had and giving it to the poor. Morally perhaps they were not required to do so, but their retention of their possessions under the patronage of the Cross made the Cross too much a sign of their possessions. "Having nothing," wrote St. Paul, "and yet possessing all things." The second clause was obvious; the first was hidden with God. A few priests, a few laymen, surrendered their lives to the needs of the destitute; the rest consoled them only with ritual prayers. The third difficulty was (briefly) philanthropy, using the word in its less bearable sense. Even those who wished to help wished also to direct. They professed a kind of paternal guardianship. Leo XIII in the very noble Encyclical *Rerum Novarum* of 1891 demanded that the capitalist should deal justly by his workers. But he also demanded that the capitalist should see that the worker "be not exposed to corrupting influences and dangerous occasions, and that he be not led away to neglect his home and family or to squander his earnings." Workers do not usually look with gratitude on employers who take care that they do not squander their earnings, or who attempt to shield them from corrupting influences. In days not then forgotten the industrial capitalist had done so by means of the tolly-system, and Disraeli's terrible and accurate pages had recorded what that meant. The receipt of a fair wage was to take with it the liberty to do as one chose with a fair wage, or it was meaningless. The Pope, no doubt, meant nothing but good. But the Pope was not a factory worker.

For all these reasons the organization of the Christian Churches, except for such bodies as the Salvation Army or such Orders as the Poor Clares, remained in the eyes of masses of men the great support of the dominant social order. "The prophets prophesied falsely and the priests bore rule by their means"; or rather the priests preached falsely and the rich bore rule by their means. "*Le bon sansculotte Jésus*" still seemed to some the prince of revolutionaries, but to more his name was the password of the black parasites of financial tyranny. The dogmas, prophecies, and fantasies of Marx sang to men as the Apocalypse had sung to them of old. The very name *Das Kapital* passed from mouth to mouth like a verse of some new and surprising love. The awakening was not confined to the Marxists. Pius XI, for example, put the matter more strongly than Leo. The population, he said, was divided into two classes. "The first, small in number, enjoyed practically all the advantages . . . the second . . . was made up of those who, oppressed by dire poverty, struggled in vain to escape from the difficulties which encompassed them. This state of things was quite satisfactory to the wealthy who looked upon it as the consequence of inevitable economic laws, and who therefore were content to leave to charity alone the full care of helping the unfortunate; as though it were the task of charity to make amends for the open violation of justice." The quotation is from the *Encyclical* of 1931. But by 1931 other things had happened, and the Church, visible and militant, was once more discovering her own message in the faces of her formal enemies.

In the east of Europe, in the dominions of that great Power which was the heir to Byzantium, a new operation and a new image had been born. Marx had done much; he had composed by one means and another a system of history, morals, and metaphysics. But he could not create the myth of Marx any more than St. Thomas could create the schools of St. Thomas. It happened. Seven centuries earlier it had been the multitudinous voices chanting the great philosophical poetry of the *Pange, lingua* which had carried the doctrine of Corpus Christi over Europe. But that Body had been too much neglected for its own praises. Now Dialectical Materialism came with something of the same fervour, and the Materialist Conception of History struck like the iron of St. Thomas's definitions. The chance (to call it that) of Lenin at the moment of the fall of the Russian throne gave the new image scope.

It was not, at first, clear. After the Revolution, while the "bourgeois" Governments were in operation, the bishops of the Russian Church met at Moscow. The Enlightenment in Russia, even more than in the West, had been confined to the upper classes in the eighteenth century, and had not been allowed to spread to the lower even in the nineteenth. There was certainly no House of Commons in Russia, but if there had been there was even less chance of a middle-class Bradlaugh forcing his way into it. Nor had the successor to the Sacred Emperors any intention of secularizing his state as the French Governments had done. As august as Rome and far more aloof than Rome, the Orthodox Church of Russia suppressed infidelity and heresy alike. A few doubtful and oppressed sects maintained a difficult life. Tolstoy might be too great in reputation to be touched, but lesser Tolstoys of the steppes were not encouraged. And in fact one had only to read Tolstoy to see with what unfortunate and sterile bitterness the Gospel of Christendom had been presented to him. So intense a genius had desired to understand the meaning of the Church, and he has told us what was offered.

The bishops met—a little disturbed but not apparently realizing the kind of danger. The Government, in accord with them, had abolished the office of Procurator of the Holy Synod, and the bishops in November 1917 reconstituted the Patriarchate of Moscow, " the third Rome." They elected a Patriarch, Tikhon. But even before then, in October, the Kerensky Government had fallen and the Bolshevik Government took their place. The Patriarch issued something like a counter-revolutionary call. The Government declared complete freedom of conscience, secularized the State and seized all the revenue-producing property of the Church. It also threw the whole of its official and unofficial influence against the Church—rather as Constantine had done on its side when he too had proclaimed complete freedom of conscience. The history of Christendom, like the personal history of Christians, is full of the remarkable fulfilments of Christ's promise to give back the full measure of what it has given. The suppressed storm of unbelief, encouraged by the new enthusiastic (and largely foreign) rejection of belief, burst upon Christendom in Russia. Images asserted to have been used to work false miracles were exhibited; priests were arrested for counter-revolutionary activities; and when in 1921, in a time of famine, the Patriarch denounced the seizure of the precious vessels used in the Rites, there existed a full persecution. God was denied with as passionate a sense of re-birth as ever he had been asserted. All over Europe men and women heard with delight that there the two-thousand years terror, the spiritual weapon of the rich, had been broken—and more, for it was not only Christianity but Religion that was being destroyed. But, locally, it was Christianity; the hideous clutch of the preachers of the crucified Jew had been torn from human life. It is not perhaps unfair to so high a sincerity, or too easy in the recollection of such great suffering, to say that in England we had heard a great deal of it before—those that read Swinburne when they were young and still remembered with pleasure those fervent romantic strains.

The dictatorship of the proletariat was declared—and liberty, to come after the usual period of transition. The " conditional " was established—on the single condition that it unconditionally denied the unconditional. The co-inherence of Communism was established. It was, as it were, the response of the opposition to the exaltation of the human Mother of God. The intended material salvation of sensuality had, inevitably, one temporal limitation; it could not redeem the past. That co-inherence could not reach the millions who had died in their misery; the Republic of the future was to be raised on their bones. That could not be helped. But the City of Christendom had declared that all must be capable of inclusion—unless indeed they deliberately preferred a perpetual exile.

The troubles settled into an uneasy and uncertain peace. The Church in Russia was partly scattered, partly suppressed, and partly in contempt allowed to return to its far fewer buildings. A disturbed and anxious Christendom was still surveying the image of the new society which had so shockingly emerged when it was distracted by the apparition of another and darker myth. The Russian persecution, however evil, had at least partly arisen from the intention of saving the poor. Its crimes, its treacheries, its tyrannies, its crusades, had come from that universal idea. If it had abolished Christianity it was, in a general sense, as willing to abolish Russia except as the headquarters of the World Revolution. Its atheist societies and its anti-God demonstrations were honestly meant to break the chains of all men, even if they broke the limbs in doing so; it would be an unfortunate result of the period of transition. But the new movement which now arose in middle Europe was not distinguished, even theoretically, by any image of a universal humanity. The Body and Blood of Christendom had been declared to be divine, human, and common; the body and blood of Communism were thought to be human and common; the body and blood of the new myth were merely German. It set itself against the very idea of the City; it raised against the world the fatalistic cry of Race. There was, no doubt, every kind of excuse; Europe had not behaved well to the Germans, nor the City to the barbarian. But whatever the cause, all Christendom in Germany felt the result. The new racial image went beyond even the Jewish exclusiveness, for it admitted no fault and it looked for no Messias; it left freedom of conscience on one point only—whether God had created the Nordic Race or whether it grew. The Race and the greatness of the Race and the Leader of the Race were its dogmas, and for those it rejected both the City of Augustus and the other City of Augustine. " It is evident, now," said one of its preachers, " that the domination of Christendom over Germanic regions was but an episode of a thousand years, a period which now belongs to the past." " The foundation of the Jewish-Christian teaching is the dogma of Original Sin," said a High School instruction. " The foundation of our heathen feeling for life is a belief in the value of healthy Blood."[7]

A thousand years before had been the Wars of the Frontiers

[7] *The Struggle for Religious Freedom in Germany,* A. S. Duncan-Jones, Dean of Chichester.

and the mass-conversions. Those times had and have returned. The masses are still being re-converted to this or that principle or god. The doctrinal advance of Christendom has been checked by doctrine. The actual frontiers, even the geographical frontiers, upon which the new wars are to be fought are not yet entirely clear, as has been recently shown in Spain. There the natural co-inherence of dogmatic Communism and the supernatural co-inherence of dogmatic Catholicism fought each other with the most intense bitterness. The one side was already murdering and destroying in the name of liberty; the other called in the Moors of Islam and the German technicians of the Healthy Blood to support the crucifixes of the Blood shed to redeem the unhealthy. So extreme, so dreadful, is the inevitable delirium of fallen man. All that is certain is that, from the point of view of Christendom, whatever comes can be but a war of frontiers. The Centre cannot be touched; all that can possibly be done has been done, outside Jerusalem, under Tiberius.

Nor has the knowledge of contrition failed. The separations in Christendom remain, nor will they be soon or easily ended. But the vocal disputes are a little suspended, and courtesies between the clamant bodies are easier; as when the Roman Catholic Paul Claudel wrote in honour of the Lutheran Niemoller—" *ce courageux confesseur de Christ.*" It might be possible now to praise the confessors of other obediences without supposing that we compromised our own; as, for example, both Donne and Dryden are acknowledged to be sincere when the one submitted to the Church of England and the other to the Church of Rome. It might be possible to " exchange " our ignorance, even if our decisions and certitudes must remain absolute. Those definitionss apart, what is there anywhere but ignorance, grace, and moral effort? Of our moral effort the less said the better; grace is always itself alone, and demands only our adoration; and therefore it is between our ignorances that our courteous Lord might cause exchange to lie, till the exchange itself became an invocation of the adorable Spirit who has so often deigned to instruct and correct the Church by voices without as well as within the Church. The last virtue which the organization of Christendom can achieve is humility, for while it is composed of members of the visible Church it always regards itself as an image of the invisible. Yet, even there, there have been moments. In 1920 the Bishops of the Church of England issued from Lambeth an " appeal to all Christian People." It was remarkable for one thing at least: for the first time a " great and sacred synod," formally convoked, formally speaking, admitted its own spiritual guilt. " It has seemed good," they said, in almost those words, " to the Holy Ghost and to us " that we should confess that we have sinned. If Christendom indeed feels intensely within itself the three strange energies which we call contrition and humility and doctrine, it will be again close, not only to the wars of the Frontiers, not only to Constantine, but to the Descent of the Dove. Its only difficulty will be to know and endure him when he comes, and that, whether it likes or not, Messias has sworn that it shall certainly do.

POSTSCRIPT

At the beginning of life in the natural order is an act of
substitution and co-inherence. A man can have no child
unless his seed is received and carried by a woman; a woman
can have no child unless she receives and carries the seed of
a man—literally bearing the burden. It is not only a mutual
act; it is a mutual act of substitution. The child itself for
nine months literally co-inheres in its mother; there is no
human creature that has not sprung from such a period of
such an interior growth.

In that natural co-inherence the Christian Church has
understood another; the about-to-be-born already co-inheres
in an ancestral and contemporary guilt. It is shapen in
wickedness, and in sin has its mother conceived it. The
fundamental fact of itself is already opposed to the principle
of the universe; it knows that good as evil, and therefore it
derives and desires its own good disorderly. It has been sown
in corruption, and in corruption it emerges into separate life.

It has been the habit of the Church to baptize it, as soon
as it has emerged, by the formula of the Trinity-in-Unity.
As it passes from the most material co-inherence it is received
into the supernatural; and it is received by a deliberate act.
The godparents present themselves as its substitutes; by
their intentions and their belief (and they are there to present
even for " those of riper years ") the new-born is granted
" that which by nature he cannot have," he is " incorporated "
into the Church, he is made " partaker " of death and resurrection. It is this co-inherence which, at the confirmation, he
himself confesses and ratifies.

The Faith into which he is received has declared that
principle to be the root and the pattern of the supernatural
as of the natural world. And the Faith is the only body
to have done so. It has proclaimed that this is due to the

deliberate choice and operation of the Divine Word. Had he willed, he could presumably have raised for his Incarnattion a body in some other way than he chose. But he preferred to shape himself within the womb, to become hereditary, to owe to humanity the flesh he divinitized by the same principle —" not by conversion of the Godhead into flesh, but by taking of the Manhood into God." By an act of substitution he reconciled the natural world with the world of the kingdom of heaven, sensuality with substance. He restored substitution and co-inherence everywhere; up and down the ladder of that great substitution all our lesser substitutions run; within that sublime co-inherence all our lesser co-inherences inhere. And when the Christian Church desired to define the nature of the Alone, she found no other term; It mutually co-inheres by Its own nature. The triune formula by which the child is baptized is precisely the incomprehensible formula of this.

It is supernatural, but also it is natural. The dreams of nationality and communism use no other language. The denunciation of individualism means this or it means nothing. The praise of individualism must allow for this or it is mere impossible anarchy. It is experienced, at their best moments of delight, by lovers and friends. It is the manner of childbirth. It is the image everywhere of supernatural charity, and the measure of this or of the refusal of this is the cause of all the images.

The apprehension of this order, in nature and in grace, without and within Christendom, should be, now, one of our chief concerns; it might indeed be worth the foundation of an Order within the Christian Church. Such a foundation would, in one sense, mean nothing, for all that it could do is already exposed and prepared, and the Church has suffered something from its interior organizations. About this there need be little organization; it could do no more than communicate an increased awareness of that duty which is part of the very nature of the Church itself. But in our present distresses, of international and social schism, among the praises of separation here or there, the pattern might be stressed, the image affirmed. The Order of the Co-inherence would exist only for that, to meditate and practise it. The principle is one of the open secrets of the saints; we might draw the smallest step nearer sanctity if we used it. Substitutions in love, exchanges in love, are a part of it; "oneself" and "others" are only the specialized terms of its technique. The technique needs much discovery; the Order would have no easy labour. But, more than can be imagined, it might find that, in this present world, its labour was never more needed, its concentration never more important, its profit never perhaps more great.

CHRONOLOGICAL TABLE[1]

[1] The earlier dates are approximate. In some of the others reputable historians vary.

354-430   Augustine
360-420   Pelagius
361-3   Julian Emperor
374   Ambrose made Bishop of Milan
379   Rule of Basil in the East
386   Conversion of Augustine
389-461   Patrick
392   Imperial prohibition of non-Christian rituals
393   Augustine made Bishop of Hippo
400   Spread of the Pelagian heresy
400   *Confessions* of Augustine
410   Fall of Rome
428   Nestorius at Byzantium
432   Patrick in Ireland
476   End of the Western Empire
529   Rule of Benedict in the West; Schools of Athens
          closed by Justinian
557   Dedication of St. Sophia
563   Columcille in Iona
570-632   Mohammed
575   Irish missions to Europe
590   Gregory the Great made Pope
622   Flight of Mohammed from Mecca
680-755   Boniface, Apostle of the Germans
717   Defeat of Islam by the Emperor Leo III
725   Edicts against Images
732   Defeat of Islam by Charles Martel
771   Charles the Great becomes King of the Franks, and
          begins the conquest of the Saxons
800   Charles crowned Emperor
842   Final Restoration of Images; Feast of Orthodoxy
867   Photius draws up articles against the West
879   Alfred defeats and baptizes the Danes
910   Foundation of Cluny
988   St. Vladimir forcibly establishes Christianity in Russia
994   St. Olaf forcibly establishes Christianity in Norway
1033-1109   Anselm

1054 Formal breach between East and West
1080-1142 Abelard
1097-9 First Crusade
1100-1200 Foundation of the Universities
1119 Founding of the Order of the Temple by nine knights
1184 Edict of Verona
1204 Sack of Byzantium
1215 Fourth Council of Lateran
1218 Dominicans established
1225-74 St. Thomas Aquinas
1233 Establishment of the Inquisition
1234 Promulgation of Canon Law
1252 Permission of torture
1259-74 *Summa Theologica*
1264 Establishment of the Feast of Corpus Christi
1265-1308 Duns Scotus
1265-1321 Dante
1270 Death of St. Louis
1300 Formal vision of the *Divine Comedy*
1302 Bull *Unam Sanctam*
1306-76 Papal residence at Avignon
1307 Arrest of the Templars
1346-8 Black Death
1373 Shewings to the Lady Julian at Norwich
1378-1417 Great Schism of the West
1430 Death of St. Joan of Arc
1440 Death of Gilles de Rais
1463 Fall of Constantinople
1486 *Malleus Maleficarum*
1490-1546 Luther
1492 Alexander VI elected Pope
1496-1556 Loyola
1509-64 Calvin
1513 Leo X elected Pope
1517 Protest against the sale of Indulgences
1521-2 Luther in seclusion
1522-3 Loyola in seclusion

1530 Diet and Confession of Augsburg

1533 Declaration of Nullity in England; birth of Elizabeth; birth of Montaigne

1534 Luther's Bible; Calvin's *Institutes;* foundation of the Society of Jesus

1542-91 St. John of the Cross

1545-63 Council of Trent

1558 Accession of Queen Elizabeth

1575-1624 Boehme

1576 First printed edition of the *Vita Nuova*

1588 Defeat of the Armada

1591 Establishment of the Patriarchate of Moscow

1592 Death of Montaigne

1593 Conversion of Henry IV of France

1623-62 Pascal

1624 *De Veritate* by Lord Herbert of Cherbury

1624-91 George Fox

1635-1705 Jansenist movement

1685 Revocation of the Edict of Nantes

1694-1778 Voltaire

1696-1787 Alphonsus Liguori

1703-1791 John Wesley

1762 Calas case in Toulouse

1773 Suppression of the Jesuits; partition of Poland

1789 Resolutions against the Slave Trade in England

1790 Civil Constitution of the Clergy in France

1813-55 Kierkegaard

1814 Restoration of the Jesuits

1818-83 Marx

1833 Oxford Movement

1837 Revival in Germany

1853 Kierkegaard's attack on the Danish Church

1854 Promulgation of the dogma of the Immaculate Conception

1858 Apparitions at Lourdes

1865 Beginnings of the Salvation Army

1867 *Das Kapital,* first volume

1870 Promulgation of the dogma of Papal Infallibility

1871-8 The *Kulturkampf*

1890-1907 *The Golden Bough*

1891 The Encyclical *Rerum Novarum*

1914 European War : first period of military operations

1917 Russian Revolution

1918 Russian decree of freedom of conscience

1920 Lambeth *Appeal to all Christian People*

1921 Persecution of the Church in Russia

1933 Nazi government in Germany

1937 Persecution of the Church in Germany

1937-9 War in Spain

1939 Euoropean War : second period of military operations

INDEX

Also from Benediction Books ...

Wandering Between Two Worlds: Essays on Faith and Art
Anita Mathias
Benediction Books, 2007
152 pages
ISBN: 0955373700

In these wide-ranging lyrical essays, Anita Mathias writes, in lush, lovely prose, of her naughty Catholic childhood in Jamshedpur, India; her large, eccentric family in Mangalore, a seacoast town converted by the Portuguese in the sixteenth century; her rebellion and atheism as a teenager in her Himalayan boarding school, run by German missionary nuns, St. Mary's Convent, Nainital; and her abrupt religious conversion after which she entered Mother Teresa's convent in Calcutta as a novice. Later rich, elegant essays explore the dualities of her life as a writer, mother, and Christian in the United States-- Domesticity and Art, Writing and Prayer, and the experience of being "an alien and stranger" as an immigrant in America, sensing the need for roots.

About the Author

Anita Mathias is the author of *Wandering Between Two Worlds: Essays on Faith and Art.* She has a B.A. and M.A. in English from Somerville College, Oxford University, and an M.A. in Creative Writing from the Ohio State University, USA. Anita won a National Endowment of the Arts fellowship in Creative Nonfiction in 1997. She lives in Oxford, England with her husband, Roy, and her daughters, Zoe and Irene.

Visit Anita at http://www.anitamathias.com.

The Church That Had Too Much
Anita Mathias
Benediction Books, 2010
52 pages
ISBN: 9781849026567

Available from www.amazon.com, www.amazon.co.uk

The Church That Had Too Much was very well-intentioned.
She wanted to love God, she wanted to love people, but she was
both hampered by her muchness and the abundance of her possessions, and beset by ambition, power struggles and snobbery.
Read about the surprising way The Church That Had Too Much
began to resolve her problems in this deceptively simple and
enchanting fable.

About the Author

Anita Mathias is the author of *Wandering Between Two
Worlds: Essays on Faith and Art.* She has a B.A. and M.A. in
English from Somerville College, Oxford University, and an
M.A. in Creative Writing from the Ohio State University, USA.
Anita won a National Endowment of the Arts fellowship in
Creative Nonfiction in 1997. She lives in Oxford, England
with her husband, Roy, and her daughters, Zoe and Irene.

Visit Anita at http://www.anitamathias.com

Francesco, Artist of Florence: The Man Who Gave Too Much
Anita Mathias
Benediction Books, 2014
52 pages (full colour)
ISBN: 978-1781394175

In this lavishly illustrated book by Anita Mathias, Francesco, artist of Florence, creates magic in pietre dure, inlaying precious stones in marble in life-like "paintings." While he works, placing lapis lazuli birds on clocks, and jade dragonflies on vases, he is purely happy. However, he must sell his art to support his family. Francesco, who is incorrigibly soft-hearted, cannot stand up to his haggling customers. He ends up almost giving away an exquisite jewellery box to Signora Farnese's bambina, who stands, captivated, gazing at a jade parrot nibbling a cherry. Signora Stallardi uses her daughter's wedding to cajole him into discounting his rainbowed marriage chest. His old friend Girolamo bullies him into letting him have the opulent table he hoped to sell to the Medici almost at cost. Carrara is raising the price of marble; the price of gems keeps rising. His wife is in despair. Francesco fears ruin.

* * *

Sitting in the church of Santa Maria Novella at Mass, very worried, Francesco hears the words of Christ. The lilies of the field and the birds of the air do not worry, yet their Heavenly Father looks after them. As He will look after us. He resolves not to worry. And as he repeats the prayer the Saviour taught us, Francesco resolves to forgive the friends and neighbours who repeatedly put their own interests above his. But can he forgive himself for his own weakness, as he waits for the eternal city of gold whose walls are made of jasper, whose gates are made of pearls, and whose foundations are sapphire, emerald, ruby and amethyst? There time and money shall be no more, the lion shall live with the lamb, and we shall dwell trustfully together. Francesco leaves Santa Maria Novella, resolving to trust the One who told him to live like the lilies and the birds, deciding to forgive those who haggled him into bad bargains--while making a little resolution for the future.